When should I travel to get the best airfare?
Where do I go for answers to my travel questions?
What's the best and easiest way to plan and book my trip?

frommers.travelocity.com

Frommer's, the travel guide leader, has teamed up with **Travelocity.com**, the leader in online travel, to bring you an in-depth, easy-to-use resource designed to help you plan and book your trip online.

At **frommers.travelocity.com**, you'll find free online updates about your destination from the experts at Frommer's plus the outstanding travel planning and purchasing features of Travelocity.com. Travelocity.com provides reservations capabilities for 95 percent of all airline seats sold, more than 47,000 hotels, and over 50 car rental companies. In addition, Travelocity.com offers more than 2,000 exciting vacation and cruise packages. Travelocity.com puts you in complete control of your travel planning with these and other great features:

> **Expert travel guidance from Frommer's** - over 150 writers reporting from around the world!

> **Best Fare Finder** - an interactive calendar tells you when to travel to get the best airfare

> **Fare Watcher** - we'll track airfare changes to your favorite destinations

> **Dream Maps** - a mapping feature that suggests travel opportunities based on your budget

> **Shop Safe Guarantee** - 24 hours a day / 7 days a week live customer service, and more!

Whether traveling on a tight budget, looking for a quick weekend getaway, or planning the trip of a lifetime, Frommer's guides and Travelocity.com will make your travel dreams a reality. You've bought the book, now book the trip!

Travelocity.com
A Sabre Company

Frommer's

Also available from Hungry Minds

Beyond Disney: The Unofficial Guide to Universal, SeaWorld, and the Best of Central Florida

Inside Disney: The Incredible Story of Walt Disney World and the Man Behind the Mouse

Mini Mickey: The Pocket-Sized Unofficial Guide to Walt Disney World

The Unofficial Guide to Bed & Breakfasts in California

The Unofficial Guide to Bed & Breakfasts in New England

The Unofficial Guide to Bed & Breakfasts in the Northwest

The Unofficial Guide to Bed & Breakfasts in the Southeast

The Unofficial Guide to Branson, Missouri

The Unofficial Guide to California with Kids

The Unofficial Guide to Chicago

The Unofficial Guide to Cruises

The Unofficial Guide to Disneyland

The Unofficial Guide to Disneyland Paris

The Unofficial Guide to Florida with Kids

The Unofficial Guide to the Great Smoky and Blue Ridge Region

The Unofficial Guide to Golf Vacations in the Eastern U.S.

The Unofficial Guide to Hawaii

The Unofficial Guide to Las Vegas

The Unofficial Guide to London

The Unofficial Guide to the Mid-Atlantic with Kids

The Unofficial Guide to New England and New York with Kids

The Unofficial Guide to New Orleans

The Unofficial Guide to New York City

The Unofficial Guide to Paris

The Unofficial Guide to San Francisco

The Unofficial Guide to Skiing in the West

The Unofficial Guide to South Florida

The Unofficial Guide to the Southeast with Kids

The Unofficial Guide to Walt Disney World

The Unofficial Guide to Walt Disney World for Grown-Ups

The Unofficial Guide to Walt Disney World with Kids

The Unofficial Guide to Washington, D.C.

The Unofficial Guide to the World's Best Diving Vacations

Mini Las Vegas

the
Pocket-Sized
Unofficial
Guide® to

Las Vegas

2nd Edition

Bob Sehlinger

Hungry Minds™

Hungry Minds, Inc.
New York, NY • Indianapolis, IN • Cleveland, OH

Please note that prices fluctuate in the course of time, and travel information changes under the impact of many factors that influence the
travel industry. We therefore suggest that you write or call ahead for confirmation when making your travel plans. Every effort has been made to
ensure the accuracy of information throughout this book and the con-
tents of this publication are believed correct at the time of printing. Nev-
ertheless, the publishers cannot accept responsibility for errors or
omissions or for changes in details given in this guide or for the conse-
quences of any reliance on the information provided by the same. Assess-
ments of attractions and so forth are based upon the author's own
experience and therefore, descriptions given in this guide necessarily
contain an element of subjective opinion, which may not reflect the
publisher's opinion or dictate a reader's own experience on another occasion. Readers are invited to write to the publisher with ideas, comments,
and suggestions for future editions

Your safety is important to us, so we encourage you to stay alert and be
aware of your surroundings. Keep a close eye on cameras, purses, and
wallets, all favorite targets of thieves and pickpockets.

Published by Hungry Minds, Inc.
909 Third Avenue
New York, NY 10022

Produced by Menasha Ridge Press

ISBN 0-7645-6234-7
ISSN 1522-3353

Manufactured in the United States of America

10 9 8 7 6 5 4 3 2 1

Contents

List of Maps and Charts

Acknowledgments

The people of Las Vegas love their city and spare no effort to assist a writer trying to dig beneath the facade of flashing neon. It is important to them to communicate that Las Vegas is a city with depth, diversity, and substance. "Don't just write about our casinos," they demand, "take the time to get to know us."

We made every effort to do just that, enabled each step of the way by some of the most sincere and energetic folks a writer could hope to encounter. Myram Borders of the Las Vegas News Bureau provided us access to anyone we wanted to see, from casino general managers to vice cops. Cam Usher of the Las Vegas Convention and Visitors Authority also spared no effort in offering assistance and contacts. Thanks to Nevada expert Deke Castleman for his contributions to our entertainment, nightlife, buffet, and hotel coverage.

Restaurant critic Muriel Stevens ate her way through dozens of new restaurants but drew the line when it came to buffet duty. Jim McDonald of the Las Vegas Police Department shared his experiences and offered valuable suggestions for staying out of trouble. Jack Sheehan evaluated Las Vegas golf courses, and forest ranger Debbie Savage assisted us in developing material on wilderness recreation.

Purple Hearts to our field research team, who chowed down on every buffet and $2 steak in town, checked in and out of countless hotels, visited tourist attractions, and stood for hours in show lines.

Much gratitude to Molly Merkle, Gabbie Oates, Russell Helms, Holly Cross, Nathan Lott, Annie Long, Dianne DiBlasi, Steve Jones, and Sylvia Coates, the pros who somehow turned all this effort into a book.

Introduction

On a Plane to Las Vegas

I never wanted to go to Las Vegas. I'm not much of a gambler and have always thought of Las Vegas as a city dedicated to separating folks from their money. As it happens, however, I have some involvement with industries that hold conventions and trade shows there. For some years I was able to persuade others to go in my place. Eventually it came my turn to go, and I found myself aboard a Delta jumbo jet on my first trip to Las Vegas.

To my surprise, I thoroughly enjoyed Las Vegas. I had a great time without gambling and have been back many times with never a bad experience. The people are friendly, the food is good, hotels are a bargain, it's an easy town to get around in, and there is plenty to do (24 hours a day, if you are so inclined).

I also discovered during my first visit that the nongambling public doesn't know very much about Las Vegas. Many people cannot see beyond the gambling, cannot see that there could possibly be anything of value in Las Vegas for nongamblers or those only marginally interested in gambling.

Las Vegas is about gambling, but there's much more. Las Vegas has mild weather two-thirds of the year, very fine hotels and restaurants, diverse celebrity and production show entertainment, unique shopping, internationally renowned golf courses, and numerous attractions. For the outdoor enthusiast, Red Rock Canyon National Conservation Area, Lake Mead National Recreation Area, and Toiyabe National Forest offer some of the most beautiful wilderness in North America.

This guide is designed for those who want to go to Las Vegas and for those who *have* to go to Las Vegas. We will show you ways to have more fun, make the most of your time, and spend less money. If you are one of the skeptics, we will demonstrate

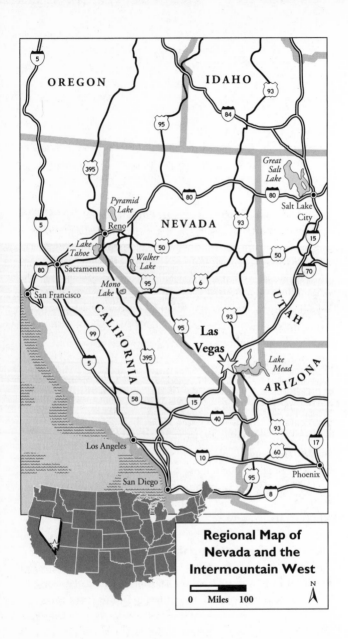

**Regional Map of
Nevada and the
Intermountain West**

0   Miles   100

N

that you can have the time of your life in this friendly city and never bet that first nickel.

About This Guide

How Come "Unofficial"?

Most "official" guides to Las Vegas tout the well-known sights, promote local casinos, restaurants, and hotels indiscriminately, and leave out a lot of good stuff. This guide is different.

Instead of pandering to the tourism industry, we'll tell you if a well-known restaurant's food is mediocre. We'll complain loudly about overpriced hotel rooms that aren't convenient to the places you want to be, and we'll guide you away from crowds and congestion.

Our evaluators toured the casinos and popular attractions, reviewed the shows, ate in the restaurants, judged hotels, and visited nightclubs. If a restaurant's food is bad or a show isn't worth the admission, we can say so—and, in the process, make your visit more fun, efficient, and economical.

Creating a Guidebook

We got into the guidebook business because we were unhappy with the way travel guides make the reader work for usable information. Most guidebooks are compilations of data presented in list form or prose. Because lists offer little detail, such guides provide little more than departure points for readers' further quests.

Many guides are readable and well researched but difficult to use. Ofetn, to select a hotel, a reader must study several pages of descriptions before narrowing their choices. If recommendations are made, they lack depth and conviction. These guides compound problems by failing to boil down travelers' choices.

How *Unofficial Guides* Are Different

Readers want the author's opinion and quick answers. This dictates that authors should be explicit, prescriptive, and direct. The *Unofficial Guides* try to do that. They spell out alternatives and recommend specific action, as well as simplifying complicated destinations and attractions and helping the traveler control unfamiliar environments. The objective of an *Unofficial Guide* is not to have the most information or all of the information, but to have the most accessible, useful, and unbiased information.

Unofficial Guide authors and researchers are completely independent from the attractions, restaurants, and hotels we describe. *Mini Las Vegas* is designed for individuals and families traveling for fun, as well as for business travelers and convention-goers, especially those visiting Las Vegas for the first time. The guide is directed at value-conscious, consumer-oriented adults.

How This Guide Was Researched and Written

Much has been written about Las Vegas, but very little of it is evaluative. Some guides regurgitate the hotels' and casinos' promotional material. In this work, we took nothing for granted. Each casino, hotel, restaurant, show, and attraction was visited at different times throughout the year by trained observers. They conducted detailed evaluations and rated each property and entertainment according to formal, pretested criteria. Tourists were interviewed to determine what visitors of all ages enjoyed most *and least.*

Observers used detailed checklists to analyze casinos, attractions, hotel rooms, buffets, and restaurants. Ratings and observations were integrated with tourists' reactions and opinions for a comprehensive quality profile of each feature and service.

Letters, Comments, and Questions from Readers

We expect to learn from our mistakes, as well as from the input of our readers, and to improve with each book and edition. Readers' comments and observations will be frequently incorporated in revised editions of the *Unofficial Guide* and will contribute immeasurably to its improvement.

How to Write the Author:

Bob Sehlinger
The Unofficial Guide to Las Vegas
P.O. Box 43673
Birmingham, AL 35243

When you write, be sure to put your return address on your letter as well as on the envelope—sometimes envelopes and letters get separated. Our work takes us out of the office for long periods of time, so our response may be delayed.

Reader Survey
At the back of this guide is a questionnaire asking about your Las Vegas visit. Mail the completed questionnaire to us.

How Information Is Organized: by Subject and by Geographic Zones
To provide fast access to information about the *best* of Las Vegas, we've organized material in several formats.

Hotels   Because most visitors stay in one hotel for the duration of their trip, our coverage of hotels is summarized in charts, maps, ratings, and rankings that allow you to quickly focus your decision-making. We concentrate on specifics that differentiate hotels: location, size, room quality, services, amenities, and cost.

Restaurants   We profile the best restaurants.

Entertainment and Nightlife   Visitors frequently try several shows or nightspots. Because these are usually selected after arrival, we offer detailed descriptions. All continuous stage shows and celebrity showrooms are reviewed. The best nightspots and lounges are profiled.

Geographic Zones   To help you locate restaurants, shows, nightspots, and attractions convenient to your hotel, we divide the city into geographic zones:

- Zone 1   The Las Vegas Strip and Environs
- Zone 2   Downtown Las Vegas
- Zone 3   Southwest Las Vegas
- Zone 4   North Las Vegas
- Zone 5   Southeast Las Vegas and the Boulder Highway

All profiles of hotels, restaurants, and nightspots include zone numbers. If, for example, you're staying at the Golden Nugget and want an Italian restaurant within walking distance, scan the restaurant profiles for restaurants in Zone 2 (downtown) for the best choices.

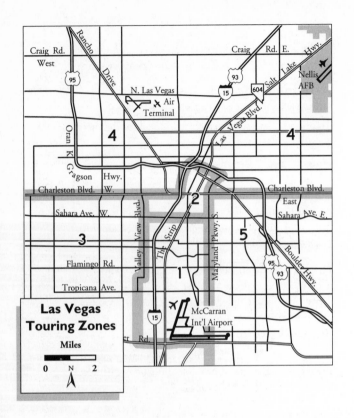

Craig Rd.
West

Craig Rd. E. Salt Lake Hwy.

95

93

15

604

Nellis
AFB

Rancho Drive

N. Las Vegas
Air
Terminal

Oran K. Gragson Hwy. W.

Las Vegas Blvd.

4

4

Charleston Blvd. W.

Charleston Blvd. East

2

Sahara Ave. W.

Sahara Ave. E.

Valley View Blvd.

The Strip

Maryland Pkwy. S.

3

5

Flamingo Rd.

1

95

Boulder Hwy.

93

Tropicana Ave.

15

McCarran
Int'l Airport

Rd.

Las Vegas
Touring Zones

Miles

0   N   2

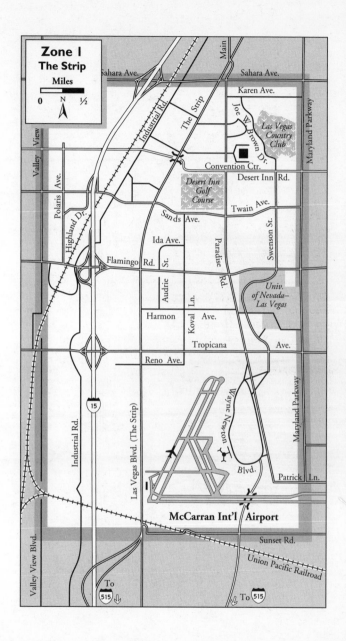

Zone 1
The Strip

Miles
0   N   ½

Sahara Ave.   Sahara Ave.

Karen Ave.

The Strip

Joe W. Brown Dr.

Las Vegas
Country
Club

Maryland Parkway

Industrial Rd.

Valley View

Valley

Polaris Ave.

Highland Dr.

Convention Ctr.

Desert Inn
Golf
Course

Desert Inn Rd.

Twain Ave.

Sands Ave.

Swenson St.

Ida Ave.

St.

Paradise Rd.

Flamingo Rd.

Audrie

Koval Ln.

Univ.
of Nevada–
Las Vegas

Harmon   Ave.

Tropicana   Ave.

Reno Ave.

I-15

Las Vegas Blvd. (The Strip)

Wayne Newton

Blvd.

Maryland Parkway

Patrick Ln.

Industrial Rd.

McCarran Int'l Airport

Valley View Blvd.

Sunset Rd.

Union Pacific Railroad

To
515

To 515

7

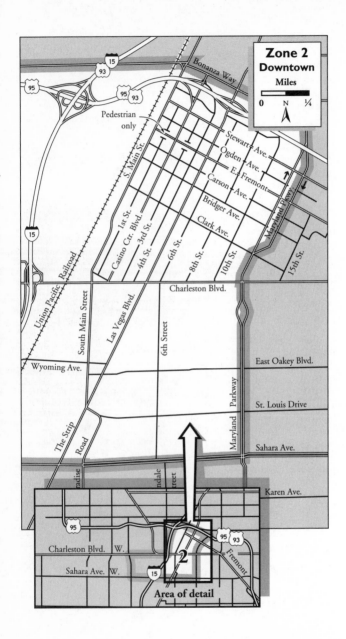

Bonanza Way

Pedestrian
only

Stewart Ave.
Ogden Ave.
E. Fremont
Carson Ave.
Bridger Ave.
Clark Ave.

S. Main St.
1st St.
Casino Ctr. Blvd.
3rd St.
4th St.
6th St.
8th St.
10th St.
15th St.

Maryland Pkwy.

Union Pacific Railroad

Charleston Blvd.

South Main Street

Las Vegas Blvd.

6th Street

East Oakey Blvd.

Wyoming Ave.

St. Louis Drive

The Strip

Maryland Parkway

Sahara Ave.

ndise Road

ndale Street

Karen Ave.

95

Charleston Blvd. W.

95   93

Sahara Ave. W.

15

2

Fremont

Area of detail

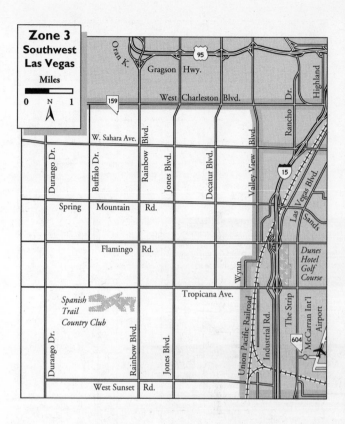

Zone 3
Southwest
Las Vegas

Miles

0   N   1

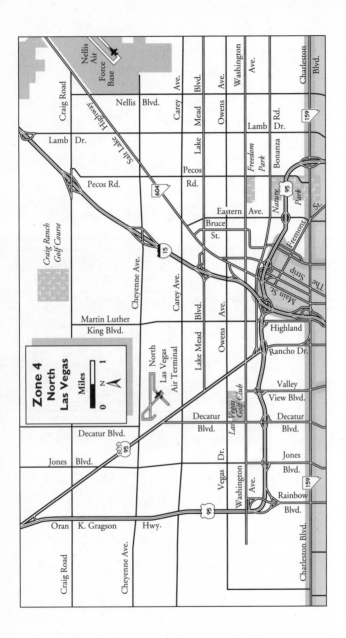

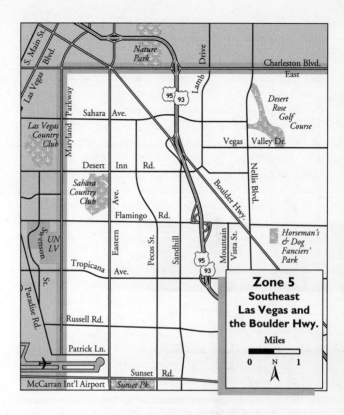

S. Main St.

Las Vegas Blvd.

Nature Park

Lamb Drive

Charleston Blvd.

East

Parkway

Sahara Ave.

Desert Rose Golf Course

Maryland

Las Vegas Country Club

Vegas Valley Dr.

Desert Inn Rd.

Nellis Blvd.

Sahara Country Club

Ave.

Flamingo Rd.

Boulder Hwy.

Swenson St.

UN LV

Eastern Ave.

Pecos St.

Sandhill

Mountain Vista St.

Horseman's & Dog Fanciers' Park

Tropicana Ave.

Paradise Rd.

Russell Rd.

Patrick Ln.

Sunset Rd.

McCarran Int'l Airport

Sunset Pk.

Zone 5
Southeast
Las Vegas and
the Boulder Hwy.

Miles

0   1

N

Las Vegas: An Overview

Gathering Information

Las Vegas has the best selection of complimentary visitor guides of any American tourist destination we know. Available at the front desk or concierge table at almost every hotel, the guides provide a wealth of useful information on gaming, gambling lessons, shows, lounge entertainment, sports, buffets, meal-deals, tours and sight-seeing, transportation, shopping, and special events. Additionally, most of the guides contain coupons for discounts on dining, shows, attractions, and tours.

What's On is the most comprehensive of the visitor guides. *Today in Las Vegas* is also very comprehensive, but is organized somewhat differently. Because both formats come in handy, we always pick up a copy of each magazine.

Other publications include *Showbiz Magazine,* published by the *Las Vegas Sun* newspaper, and *Where Las Vegas.* Both have much of the information discussed above plus feature articles.

The *Las Vegas Advisor* is a 12-page monthly newsletter containing some of the most useful consumer information available on gaming, dining, and entertainment, as well as taking advantage of deals on rooms, drinks, shows, and meals. With no advertising or promotional content, the newsletter serves its readers with objective, prescriptive, no-nonsense advice, presented with a sense of humor. At a subscription rate of $50 a year, the *Las Vegas Advisor* is the best investment you can make if you plan to spend four or more days in Las Vegas each year. If you are a one-time visitor but wish to avail yourself of all this wisdom, single copies of the *Las Vegas Advisor* can be purchased for $5 at the Gambler's Book Club store at 630 South 11th Street, (702) 382-7555. To speed delivery of the first issue (which includes discount coupons), send a self-addressed, legal-sized envelope with 77 cents postage along with your request. For additional information, write:

Las Vegas Advisor
Huntington Press
3687 South Procyon Ave., Suite A
Las Vegas, NV 89103
(702) 252-0655 or (800) 244-2224
www.lasvegasadvisor.com

Las Vegas and the Internet

The explosive growth of Las Vegas is not only physical, but also virtual. Three years ago at this time, Las Vegas casinos had a minimal presence on the world wide web; this year, there are too many sites to list. The following are the best places to go on the web to launch yourself into Las Vegas cyberspace. Use the directories to surf the many individual sites.

The official website of the Las Vegas Convention and Visitors Authority is www.lasvegas24hours.com.

For the largest selection of Las Vegas casinos on the web, look up www.intermind.net, then hit Hotels & Casinos.

A site aimed at people relocating to Las Vegas or interested in investing in Las Vegas real estate is at www.lasvegas4sale.com.

Other Las Vegas on-ramps include:

www.vegas.com
www.lasvegas.com
www.pcap.com
www.casinogambling.about.com
www.lasvegasadvisor.com
www.ilovevegas.com

When to Go to Las Vegas

The best time to go to Las Vegas is spring or fall, when the weather is pleasant (see weather/dress chart on p. 22). If you plan to be indoors, it doesn't matter when you go. Spring and fall are the most popular, but the best deals are in December (after the National Finals Rodeo in early December and excluding the week between Christmas and New Year's), January, and during summer, particularly July and August.

Weather in December, January, and February can vary incredibly, but chances are better than even that temperatures will be moderate and the sun will shine. Winter provides an unbeatable combination of good value and choice of activities. From mid-May through mid-September, the heat is blistering.

Crowd Avoidance

Weekends generally are busy; weekdays, slower. Exceptions are holiday periods and when large conventions or special events are being held. (Two or three concurrent medium-sized conventions can impact Las Vegas as much as one citywide event.) Most hotels' rates are lower on weekdays. For a stress-free arrival at the

		Las Vegas Weather and Dress Chart		
Month	Average a.m. Temp.	Average p.m. Temp.	Pools O=Open	Recommended Attire
January	57	32		Coats and jackets are a must.
February	50	37		Dress warmly: jackets and sweaters.
March	69	42	O	Sweaters for days, but a jacket at night.
April	78	50	O	Still cool at night—bring a jacket.
May	88	50	O	Sweater for evening, but days are warm.
June	99	68	O	Days hot and evenings are moderate.
July	105	75	O	Bathing suits.
August	102	73	O	Dress for the heat—spend time at a pool!
September	95	65	O	Days warm, sweater for evening.
October	81	53	O	Bring a jacket or sweater for afternoon.
November	67	40		Sweaters and jackets, coats for night.
December	58	34		Coats and jackets a must: dress warmly!

airport, good availability of rental cars, and quick hotel check-in, arrive Monday afternoon through Thursday morning (Tuesday and Wednesday are best).

Las Vegas hosts huge conventions and special events (rodeos, prizefights) that tie up hotels, restaurants, transportation, show-rooms, and traffic for a week at a time. For a complete convention calendar, call the Las Vegas Convention and Visitors Authority at (702) 892-0711.

Arriving and Getting Oriented

If you drive, you will cross the desert to reach Las Vegas. Make sure your car is in good shape, and carry a couple of gallons of water for emergencies. Monitor fuel and temperature gauges.

Virtually all commercial air traffic uses McCarran International Airport, a well-designed facility with clear signs. You will have no problem navigating, but the walk to baggage claim can be long. Baggage handling is slow. While your checked luggage is en route, complete paperwork at nearby car rental counters. Have your baggage claim check handy; you'll have to show it.

Not renting a car? No problem. Shuttles to hotels start at $4.50 one way and $9 round trip. Sedans and "stretch" limousines cost about $28 to $35 one way. Cabs are also available; the fare to Strip locations is about $9 to $18 one way, plus tip. A cab to downtown is about $16 to $23 one way. Limo service counters are just outside baggage claim; cabs are at the curb.

If you rent a car, catch your rental company's courtesy vehicle at the middle curb of the authorized vehicle lanes (ground level between the baggage claim building and the terminal).

If someone is picking you up, proceed on ground level to the opposite side of the baggage claim building (away from the main terminal) to the baggage claim/arrivals curb. If the person picking you up wants to park, meet on the ground level of the baggage claim building near the car rental counters where the escalators descend from the main terminal.

By car, leave the airport via Swenson Street, which runs north-south roughly paralleling the Strip, or take the spur of I-515, which connects with I-15. We recommend I-515 if you're

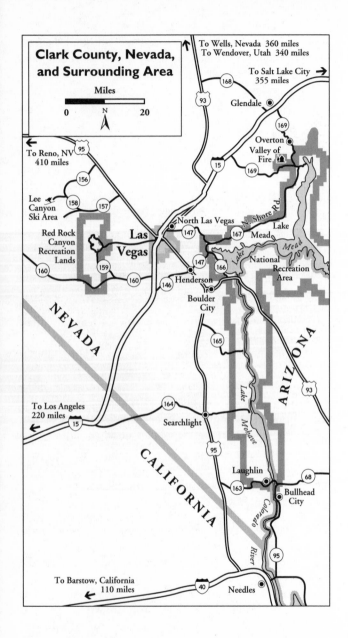

Clark County, Nevada, and Surrounding Area

Miles

0   20

N

To Wells, Nevada 360 miles
To Wendover, Utah 340 miles

To Salt Lake City
355 miles

168

93

Glendale

169

Overton

Valley of
Fire

15

169

To Reno, NV
410 miles

95

156

158

Lee
Canyon
Ski Area

157

North Las Vegas

147

N. Shore Rd.

167

Lake
Mead

Las
Vegas

Red Rock
Canyon
Recreation
Lands

159

147

166

Lake Mead

Lake Mead
National
Recreation
Area

160

160

Henderson

146

Boulder
City

NEVADA

165

To Los Angeles
220 miles

15

164

Searchlight

95

Lake Mohave

ARIZONA

93

CALIFORNIA

Laughlin

163

68

Bullhead
City

Colorado

95

To Barstow, California
110 miles

40

Needles

River

16

headed downtown or to hotels west of the Strip. Swenson Street is better if you're going to the Las Vegas Convention Center, UNLV, or hotels on or east of the Strip.

Convenience Chart   In Part One, we've included a chart of estimated times by foot and cab from major hotels to popular destinations plus tips for avoiding traffic between the Strip and downtown.

Rental Cars   All national car rental companies and a few local firms serve the city. Agencies with counters at McCarran process customers faster than do off-airport sites, which also require a commute to their location. (Courtesy vehicles pick up at the center curb outside baggage claim.) The county charges 8% of your rental fee if you use an off-airport agency. With 7% sales tax, 6% state surcharge, and 8% airport fee, rental car taxes can add 21% to your bill.

Prices fluctuate; have your travel agent check rates at all rental agencies for the dates of your visit. On many weekends or when a citywide convention is in town, rental cars may be unavailable unless you reserve in advance. When business is slow, rentals may go for as little as $22 a day. In slow seasons, reserve ahead but check each company on arrival. You may find a better deal.

When you or your travel agent reserve a rental car, ask for the smallest and least expensive (you may be upgraded without charge on arrival). Or, agencies frequently offer on-site upgrades that beat advance deals. Always compare daily and weekly rates.

If you decline insurance coverage on the rental car, be clear what protection your credit card provides and how your regular auto insurance covers you. In most cases, credit card coverage reimburses you only the deductible on your regular policy. If you decline coverage, inspect the vehicle very carefully for any damage (even a windshield nick) and have the agent record any blemish. Among credit cards, Diner's Club offers the best supplemental coverage.

Some agencies require that you drive only in Nevada. If you visit Hoover Dam or the Grand Canyon, you will cross into Arizona. Also, your agency may charge for additional drivers.

Return the car with a full gas tank. Some companies charge $3 or more per gallon for gas.

RENTAL CAR AGENCIES

AT THE TERMINAL	OFF-AIRPORT
Airport Car Rental	Alamo
All State	Enterprise
Avis	Ladki International
Budget	Practical
Dollar	Resort
Hertz	Thrifty
National	US Rent-A-Car
Savmor	

Public Transportation   Las Vegas's Citizen's Area Transit (CAT) provides reliable bus service at reasonable rates. One-way fares along the Strip are $1.25. Children ages five and younger ride free. Exact fare is required. Transfers are free but must be used within two hours of issue. Handicapped persons requiring door-to-door service should call ahead for reservations. For more details, call (702) 228-4800. For general information call (702) 228-7433.

The privately owned Las Vegas Strip Trolley Company provides transportation on the Strip and between the Strip and downtown. Its buses mimic San Francisco cable cars, and the fare is $1.10. Children ages four and younger ride free. Call (702) 382-1404 for information.

Las Vegas Customs and Protocol

The only rules for being accepted in Las Vegas are these: Have a shirt on your back, shoes on your feet, clothing below the waist, and money in your pocket (the minimum is fare back to wherever you came from).

After that, there are three areas where the uninitiated feel insecure:

Gambling   Despite appearances, gambling is very informal. It's smart to avoid a game you don't know how to play, but uncertainty over the protocol shouldn't stop you. What little protocol exists (including holding your cards above the table and keeping your hands away from your bet once play has begun) has evolved to protect the house and honest players from cheats. Dealers (those who conduct table games) aren't ordered to be unfriendly or silent. Before you sit down, find a game that interests you and observe that the dealer is personable and polite. Never play where the staff is surly; life's too short.

Eating in Gourmet Restaurants   Don't be intimidated. These are mostly meat and potatoes places with fancy names. Men will feel more comfortable in sport coats; ties are optional. Women wear everything from slacks to evening attire. When you sit down, a platoon of waiters will attend you. Let the waiter put your napkin in your lap. Then, the senior waiter speaks. Afterward, you may order cocktails, consider the menu, sip your water, or converse. Women in a mixed party will receive a menu without prices. In an all-woman party, a menu with prices will be given to the woman who looks oldest.

There will be enough utensils on the table to perform surgery. Use a different one for each dish, and let the waiter take it at the end of the course. Small yellow sculptures are probably butter.

Tipping   Las Vegas has no scarcity of people to tip. Remember that a tip isn't automatic—it rewards good service. Here are traditional amounts:

Porters and Redcaps   A dollar a bag.

Cab Drivers   A lot depends on the service and the courtesy. If the fare is less than $8, give the cabbie the change and $1. On a $4.50 fare, in other words, give him the 50 cents change plus a buck. If the fare is more than $8, give the cabbie the change and $2. If you are asking the cabbie to take you only a block or two, the fare will be small, but your tip should be large ($3–5) to make up for his wait in line and to partially compensate him for missing a better-paying fare. Add an extra dollar to your tip if the cabbie does a lot of luggage handling.

Valet Parking   Two dollars is correct if the valet is courteous and demonstrates some hustle. A dollar will do if the service is just OK. Only pay when you take your car out, not when you leave it. Because valet attendants pool their tips, both of the individuals who assist you (coming and going) will be taken care of.

Bellmen   When a bellhop greets you at your car with one of those rolling carts and handles all of your bags, $5 is about right.

The more of your luggage that you carry, of course, the less you should tip.

Waiters   Whether in a coffee shop, a gourmet room, or ordering from room service, the standard gratuity for acceptable service is 15% of the total tab, before sales tax. At a buffet or brunch where you serve yourself, it is customary to leave $1–2 for the folks who bring your drinks and bus your dishes.

Cocktail Waiters/Bartenders   Here you tip by the round. For two people, $1 a round; for more than two people, $2 a round. For a large group, use your judgment: Is everyone drinking beer, or is the order long and complicated? In casinos where drinks are free, tip the server $1 per round or every couple of rounds.

Dealers and Slot Attendants   If you are winning, it is a nice gesture to tip the dealer or place a small bet for him. How much depends on your winnings and on your level of play. With slot attendants, tip when they perform a specific service or when you hit a jackpot. In general, unless other services are also rendered, it is not customary to tip change makers or cashiers.

Keno Runners   Tip if you have a winner or if the runner really provides fast, efficient service. How much to tip will vary with your winnings and with your level of play.

Showroom Maître d's, Captains, and Servers   If you are planning to take in a show, see our suggestions for tipping in the chapter on entertainment (see page 85).

Hotel Maids   On checking out, leave $1–2 for each day you stayed, providing the service was good.

Does Anyone Know What's Going on at Home? (Does Anyone Really Care?)

Borders Book Shop at 2323 South Decatur Boulevard stocks Sunday papers from most major cities. To find out whether Borders stocks your favorite newspaper, call (702) 258-0999.

Las Vegas as a Family Destination

Occasionally the publisher sends me around to promote the *Unofficial Guide* on radio and television, and every year I am asked the same question: Is Las Vegas a good place for a family vacation?

Objectively speaking, Las Vegas is a great place for a family vacation. Food and lodging are a bargain, and there are an extraordinary number of things, from swimming at Wet 'n Wild to rafting through the Black Canyon on the Colorado River, that the entire family can enjoy together. If you take your kids to Las Vegas *and forget gambling,* Las Vegas compares favorably with every family tourist destination in the United States. The rub, of course, is that gambling in Las Vegas is pretty hard to ignore.

Marketing gurus, as you may have observed, have tried mightily to recast the town's image and to position Las Vegas as a family destination. The strategy no doubt attracts some parents already drawn to gambling but previously unwilling to allocate family vacation time to a Las Vegas trip. Excepting these relatively few families, however, it takes a lot more than hype to convince most parents that Las Vegas is a suitable destination for a family vacation.

For years, Las Vegas has been touted as a place to *get away* from your kids. For family tourism to succeed in Las Vegas, that characterization has to be changed, or at least minimized. Next, and much more unlikely, gambling must be relegated to a position of secondary importance. There is gambling on cruise ships, for example, but gambling is not the primary reason people go on cruises. Las Vegas, similarly, cannot develop as a bona fide family destination until something supersedes gambling as the main draw. Not very likely.

To legitimately appeal to the family travel market, the city must consider the real needs of children and parents. Instead of banishing children to midway and electronic games arcades, hotels need to offer substantive, educational, supervised programs or "camps" for children. The Station casinos are breaking some new ground in this area. Additionally, and equally important, Las Vegas must target and sell the family tourist trade in nontraditional geographic markets. Though Southern California is Las Vegas's largest and most lucrative market, it's not reasonable to expect families with nearby Disneyland, SeaWorld, and Universal Studios to go to Las Vegas to visit a theme park.

Tours and Excursions

For the most part, the various bus sight-seeing tours available in Las Vegas offer two things: transportation and drivers who know where they're going. In our opinion, if you have a car and can read a map, you will save both money and hassle by going on your own.

Special Events

There is almost always something fun going on in Las Vegas outside of gambling. Among other things, there are minor league baseball, rodeos, concerts, UNLV basketball and football, and, of course, movies. If you are traveling with children, it's worth the effort to pick up a local newspaper and check out what's going on.

Part One

Lodging and Casinos

Where to Stay: Basic Choices

The Las Vegas Strip and Downtown

From a visitor's perspective, Las Vegas is a small town and fairly easy to navigate. Most major hotels and casinos are in two areas: downtown and on Las Vegas Boulevard, known as the Strip.

Downtown hotels and casinos are generally older and smaller than those on the Strip, but there are large and elegant hotels downtown. What differentiates downtown is the incredible concentration of casinos and hotels in a relatively small area. Along four blocks of Fremont Street, downtown's main thoroughfare, the casinos present a dazzling galaxy of neon and twinkling lights known as Glitter Gulch. Several dozen casinos are sandwiched into an area barely larger than the parking lot at a good-sized shopping mall.

Downtown has the atmosphere of New Orleans's Bourbon Street: alluring, exotic, wicked, sultry, foreign, and, above all, diverse. It's where cowboy, businessperson, showgirl, and retiree mix easily. And like Bourbon Street, it's accessible on foot.

If downtown is the French Quarter, then the Strip is Plantation Row. At its heart, huge hotel-casinos sprawl like estates along four miles of Las Vegas Boulevard South. Each hotel is a vacation destination unto itself, with casino, hotel, restaurants, pools, spas, landscaped grounds, and even golf courses.

Considered part of the Strip is the Paradise Road area east and parallel to the Strip where the Las Vegas Convention Center and several hotels are located. Also included are hotels and casinos on streets intersecting Las Vegas Boulevard, and properties immediately west of the Strip (far side of I-15).

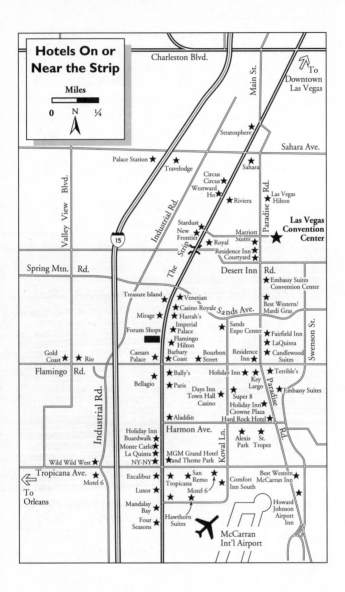

Hotels On or Near the Strip

Miles

0   N   ¼

Charleston Blvd.

Main St.

To Downtown Las Vegas

Stratosphere ★

Sahara Ave.

Palace Station ★   ★ Travelodge

Circus Circus ★

Westward Ho ★

Sahara ★

Riviera ★

Las Vegas Hilton ★

Valley View Blvd.

Industrial Rd.

15

Stardust ★
New Frontier ★

★ Royal

Marriott Suites ★

Las Vegas Convention Center ★

The Strip

Residence Inn ★
Courtyard ★

Paradise Rd.

Spring Mtn. Rd.

Desert Inn   Rd.

★ Embassy Suites
Convention Center

Treasure Island ★

★ Venetian

★ Casino Royale   Sands Ave.

★ Best Western/
Mardi Gras

Mirage ★   ★ Harrah's

Forum Shops

★ Imperial Palace

Sands Expo Center

★ Fairfield Inn

Swenson St.

★ Flamingo Hilton

★ LaQuinta

Gold Coast ★   ★ Rio

Caesars Palace ★

Barbary Coast ★

Bourbon Street ★

Residence Inn ★

★ Candlewood Suites

Flamingo Rd.

Bellagio ★

★ Bally's

Holiday Inn ★ ★

★ Terrible's

★ Paris

Days Inn ★
Town Hall Casino ★

Key Largo ★

★ Embassy Suites

Super 8 ★

Industrial Rd.

★ Aladdin

Holiday Inn ★
Crowne Plaza
Hard Rock Hotel ★

Harmon Ave.

Koval Ln.

Alexis Park ★

★ St. Tropez

Holiday Inn Boardwalk ★
Monte Carlo ★
La Quinta ★
NY-NY ★

MGM Grand Hotel and Theme Park ★

Wild Wild West ★

Tropicana Ave. ★
Motel 6

To Orleans

Excalibur ★

Luxor ★

★ San Remo ★
Tropicana ★
Motel 6 ★

Comfort Inn South ★

Best Western ★
McCarran Inn

Mandalay Bay ★

Four Seasons ★

Hawthorn Suites ★

McCarran Int'l Airport

Howard Johnson Airport Inn ★

The Strip vs. Downtown for Leisure Travelers

Although there are excellent hotels on the Boulder Highway and elsewhere, most vacationers stay downtown or on/near the Strip. Downtown offers a good range of hotels, restaurants, and gambling, but only limited entertainment and fewer amenities such as swimming pools. By car, the Strip is 8 to 15 minutes from downtown via I-15. If you don't have a car, public transportation to the Strip is affordable and as efficient as traffic allows.

If you stay on the Strip, you're more likely to need a car or other transportation. Hotels are spread out and often pricier than downtown. Entertainment is varied and extensive, and recreational facilities rival the world's best.

Downtown is a multicultural melting pot with an adventurous, raw, robust feel. Everything seems intense and concentrated, a blur of action and light.

Although downtown caters to every class of clientele, it's less formal and generally a working man's venue. The Strip runs the gamut but tends to attract more high rollers, suburbanites, and business travelers.

If You Visit Las Vegas on Business

If you're going to Las Vegas for a trade show or convention, lodge as near as possible to the meeting site, ideally within walking distance. Many Strip hotel-casinos are convenient to citywide shows and conventions at the Las Vegas Convention Center and have good track records with business travelers. Our maps will help you pinpoint lodging near your meeting site.

Citywide conventions often provide shuttles between major hotels and the Convention Center, and cabs are also available.

Large Hotel-Casinos vs. Small Hotels and Motels

If your itinerary calls for a car and a lot of coming and going, big hotels can be a pain. At the Luxor, Excalibur, and Las Vegas Hilton, for example, it can take 15 minutes to reach your room from your car if you self-park. If you plan to use the car frequently, stay in a smaller lodging with convenient parking.

Many visitors object to passing through a noisy, round-the-clock casino to reach their room. Staying at smaller properties without a casino eliminates this problem.

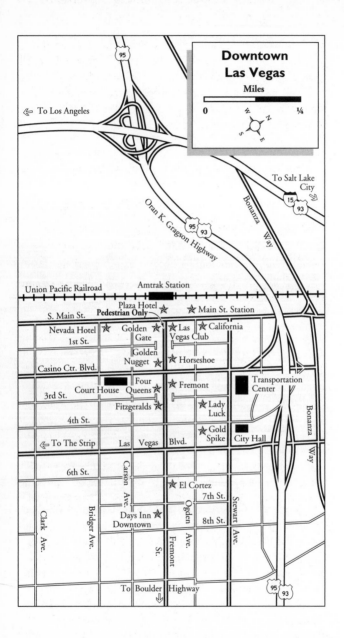

Downtown Las Vegas

Miles

0   ¼

To Los Angeles

To Salt Lake City

Bonanza Way

Oran K. Gragson Highway

Union Pacific Railroad   Amtrak Station

Plaza Hotel ★   ★ Main St. Station
S. Main St.   **Pedestrian Only**

Nevada Hotel   ★   Golden ★   ★ Las   ★ California
1st St.   Gate   Vegas Club

                        Golden
Casino Ctr. Blvd.   Nugget ★   ★ Horseshoe

                         Four
3rd St.   Court House   Queens ★   ★ Fremont

              Fitzgeralds ★   ★ Lady
4th St.   Luck

To The Strip   Las Vegas Blvd.   ★ Gold   City Hall
                                        Spike

6th St.

                                  ★ El Cortez
                                      7th St.

Carson Ave.   Days Inn ★
                   Downtown   8th St.

Clark Ave.   Bridger Ave.   Ogden Ave.   Stewart Ave.   Bonanza Way

                         Fremont St.

Transportation Center

To Boulder Highway

More comfortable or luxurious rooms aren't a certainty at large hotels. Any lodging can be threadbare or poorly designed. A large hotel, however, usually ensures superior amenities.

If you plan to tour mostly on foot or are attending a convention, a large hotel in a good location has the edge. If you want to immerse yourself in the atmosphere of Las Vegas, book a large hotel.

Getting Around: Location and Convenience

Las Vegas Lodging Convenience Chart

The following chart indicates how convenient a sampling of lodgings are to common destinations. Times are conservative.

COMMUTING TIME IN MINUTES

From: Hotel	To: Las Vegas Strip	Convention Center	Down- town	McCarran Airport	UNLV Thomas & Mack Center
Aladdin	on Strip	8/cab	15/cab	7/cab	8/cab
Alexis Park	5/cab	8/cab	15/cab	5/cab	6/cab
Bally's	on Strip	8/cab	15/cab	7/cab	7/cab
Bellagio	on Strip	12/cab	15/cab	11/cab	12/cab
Best Western	6/cab	9/cab	15/cab	4/cab	7/cab
Bourbon Street	4/walk	8/cab	15/cab	7/cab	7/cab
Caesars Palace	on Strip	10/cab	12/cab	10/cab	10/cab
California	13/cab	15/cab	downtown	19/cab	19/cab
Castaways	19/cab	18/cab	12/cab	21/cab	20/cab
Circus Circus	on Strip	5/cab	13/cab	14/cab	13/cab
Comfort Inn	3/cab	9/cab	15/cab	4/cab	6/cab
Courtyard	4/cab	5/walk	15/cab	9/cab	8/cab
El Cortez	11/cab	15/cab	6/walk	16/cab	17/cab
Excalibur	on Strip	13/cab	14/cab	7/cab	8/cab
E-Z 8 Motel	4/cab	9/cab	12/cab	9/cab	10/cab
Fiesta Hotel	18/cab	18/cab	10/cab	22/cab	22/cab
Fitzgeralds	14/cab	15/cab	downtown	17/cab	17/cab
Flamingo Hilton	on Strip	9/cab	13/cab	8/cab	8/cab
Four Queens	15/cab	15/cab	downtown	19/cab	17/cab

COMMUTING TIME IN MINUTES (continued)

Hotel	Las Vegas Strip	Convention Center	Down-town	McCarran Airport	UNLV Thomas & Mack Center
Four Seasons	on Strip	14/cab	15/cab	7/cab	13/cab
Fremont	15/cab	15/cab	downtown	19/cab	17/cab
Frontier	on Strip	8/cab	13/cab	11/cab	10/cab
Golden Nugget	14/cab	15/cab	downtown	18/cab	19/cab
Green Valley Ranch Station	15/cab	18/cab	16/cab	15/cab	14/cab
Hard Rock Hotel	4/cab	6/cab	15/cab	6/cab	6/cab
Harrah's	on Strip	9/cab	15/cab	10/cab	10/cab
Holiday Inn Crowne Plaza	5/cab	5/cab	14/cab	8/cab	6/cab
Holiday Inn Emerald Springs	4/cab	8/cab	15/cab	7/cab	7/cab
Horseshoe	14/cab	15/cab	downtown	19/cab	19/cab
Howard Johnson	4/cab	14/cab	14/cab	9/cab	11/cab
Imperial Palace	on Strip	9/cab	15/cab	10/cab	10/cab
Lady Luck	14/cab	15/cab	3/walk	19/cab	18/cab
Las Vegas Hilton	5/cab	5/walk	13/cab	10/cab	8/cab
Luxor	on Strip	13/cab	15/cab	8/cab	10/cab
Mandalay Bay	on Strip	14/cab	16/cab	7/cab	13/cab
Marriott Suites	14/cab	5/walk	15/cab	10/cab	9/cab
MGM Grand	on Strip	12/cab	15/cab	9/cab	9/cab
Mirage	on Strip	11/cab	15/cab	11/cab	10/cab
Monte Carlo	on Strip	12/cab	15/cab	11/cab	12/cab
New York–New York	on Strip	12/cab	15/cab	11/cab	12/cab
Orleans	4/cab	15/cab	14/cab	11/cab	11/cab
Palace Station	5/cab	10/cab	10/cab	14/cab	15/cab
Palm	5/cab	13/cab	14/cab	10/cab	10/cab
Paris	on Strip	9/cab	15/cab	8/cab	8/cab
Plaza Hotel	14/cab	15/cab	downtown	19/cab	18/cab
Regent Las Vegas	18/cab	21/cab	15/cab	23/cab	24/cab
Reserve	18/cab	17/cab	19/cab	17/cab	15/cab
Rio	5/cab	14/cab	13/cab	10/cab	10/cab
Riviera	on Strip	4/cab	14/cab	11/cab	10/cab
Sahara	on Strip	4/cab	13/cab	13/cab	11/cab

COMMUTING TIME IN MINUTES (continued)

Hotel	Las Vegas Strip	Convention Center	Down-town	McCarran Airport	UNLV Thomas & Mack Center
St. Tropez	5/cab	6/cab	15/cab	7/cab	6/cab
Sam's Town	20/cab	25/cab	20/cab	18/cab	17/cab
Santa Fe Station	27/cab	30/cab	23/cab	33/cab	36/cab
Silverton	10/cab	17/cab	20/cab	12/cab	17/cab
Stardust	on Strip	4/cab	13/cab	12/cab	10/cab
Stratosphere	3/cab	7/cab	9/cab	14/cab	14/cab
Sunset Station	18/cab	17/cab	18/cab	16/cab	15/cab
Terrible's	5/cab	6/cab	15/cab	6/cab	6/cab
Texas Station	17/cab	16/cab	13/cab	22/cab	22/cab
Treasure Island	on Strip	11/cab	14/cab	11/cab	10/cab
Tropicana	on Strip	11/cab	15/cab	6/cab	9/cab
Vacation Village	8/cab	18/cab	18/cab	8/cab	12/cab
Venetian	on Strip	9/cab	14/cab	8/cab	8/cab

Commuting to Downtown from the Strip

From the Strip, access I-15 at Tropicana Avenue, Flamingo Road, Spring Mountain Road, or Sahara Avenue. Northbound on I-15, keep right and follow signs for downtown and US 95 South. Exit onto Casino Center Boulevard, and you'll be right in the middle of downtown convenient to large parking garages. Driving time varies between 14 minutes from the south end of the Strip (I-15 via Tropicana Avenue) to about 6 minutes from the north end (I-15 via Sahara Avenue).

Commuting to the Strip from Downtown

From downtown, pick up US 95 (and then I-15) by going north on either Fourth Street or Las Vegas Boulevard. Driving time is 6–14 minutes, depending on your destination.

Free Connections

Traffic on the Strip is so awful that the hotels, both individually and in groups, are creating new alternatives for getting around.

1. A monorail connects Bally's, Paris Las Vegas, and the MGM Grand on the east side of the Strip, while an

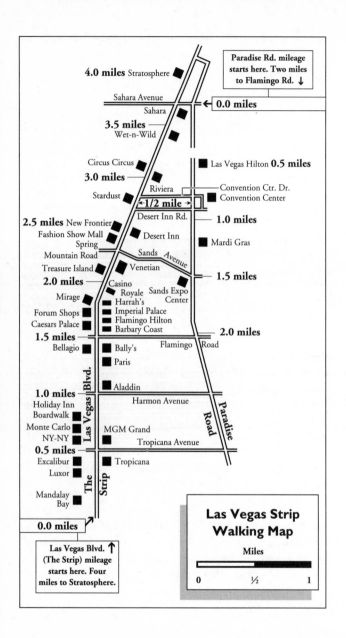

4.0 miles Stratosphere

Paradise Rd. mileage
starts here. Two miles
to Flamingo Rd. ↓

Sahara Avenue

← **0.0 miles**

Sahara

3.5 miles —
Wet-n-Wild

Circus Circus

■ Las Vegas Hilton **0.5 miles**

3.0 miles —

Stardust

Riviera

Convention Ctr. Dr.
Convention Center

← **1/2 mile** →

Desert Inn Rd.

1.0 miles

2.5 miles New Frontier

Fashion Show Mall
Spring
Mountain Road

Desert Inn

Sands Avenue

■ Mardi Gras

Treasure Island

1.5 miles

Venetian

2.0 miles —

Casino
Royale

Sands Expo
Center

Mirage

Harrah's

Forum Shops

Imperial Palace

Caesars Palace

Flamingo Hilton

1.5 miles —

Barbary Coast

2.0 miles —

Bellagio

Bally's

Flamingo Road

Paris

Aladdin

1.0 miles —

Harmon Avenue

Holiday Inn
Boardwalk

Monte Carlo

MGM Grand

NY-NY

Tropicana Avenue

0.5 miles —

Excalibur

Tropicana

Luxor

Mandalay
Bay

Las Vegas Blvd.

The Strip

Paradise Road

0.0 miles

Las Vegas Blvd. ↑
(The Strip) mileage
starts here. Four
miles to Stratosphere.

Las Vegas Strip
Walking Map

Miles

0   ½   1

elevated tram (that looks like a monorail) links Bellagio and Monte Carlo on the west side. Farther south on the west side, a shuttle tram serves Excalibur, Luxor, Mandalay Bay, and Four Seasons.

2. The Rio operates a shuttle from the Rio Visitor's Center to the Rio. Shuttles also link Barbary Coast on the northeast corner of the Strip and Flamingo to the Gold Coast about a mile west.

3. Free shuttle service from the nongaming Polo Towers near the Aladdin to the Stratosphere runs on the hour northbound to the Stratosphere and on the half hour for the southbound return from 9 a.m. until 11 p.m.

What's in an Address?

Downtown

The heart of the downtown casino area is Fremont Street between Fourth Street (on the east) and Main Street (on the west). Hotel-casinos on this quarter-mile called Glitter Gulch include the Plaza Hotel, Golden Gate, Las Vegas Club, Binion's Horseshoe, Golden Nugget, Sam Boyd's Fremont, Four Queens, and Fitzgeralds. Parallel to Fremont and one block north on Ogden Avenue are the California, Lady Luck, and the Gold Spike. Main Street Station is on Main Street at the Ogden intersection.

Although hotel quality and price vary greatly downtown, all properties are convenient to the action. The exception is El Cortez, three blocks east.

The Strip

Location is of paramount importance on the Strip. Some promotional photographs make the Strip look compact. But the Strip is about seven miles long, running from southwest of the airport to downtown. Only the four miles between Mandalay Bay and the Stratosphere contain the large casinos and other visitor attractions.

The Best Locations on the Strip

Beware of hotels and motels claiming to be on the Strip but not located between Mandalay Bay and the Stratosphere. Their location will disappoint you.

Some Strip sections are preferable. The south anchor Mandalay Bay is a quarter-mile from Luxor, its closest neighbor. The Stratosphere and the Sahara are somewhat isolated at the other end. In between are distinct clusters of hotels and casinos.

Strip Cluster 1: The Cluster of the Giants   At the intersection of the Strip and Tropicana Avenue are five of the world's largest hotels. The MGM Grand Hotel is the largest U.S. hotel. Diagonally across from the MGM Grand is Excalibur, the third-largest hotel in the United States. The other two corners are occupied by New York–New York and the Tropicana. To the south is Luxor (second largest), and north are the Holiday Inn Boardwalk and Monte Carlo. The San Remo is on Tropicana across from the MGM Grand. The next cluster of major hotels and casinos is one mile north at Flamingo Road.

Strip Cluster 2: The Grand Cluster   From Flamingo Road to Spring Mountain Road (also called Sands Avenue, and farther east, Twain Avenue) lies the greatest concentration of major hotels and casinos. If you want to stay on the Strip and prefer to walk wherever you go, this is the best location. At Flamingo Road and Las Vegas Boulevard are Bally's, Caesars Palace, Barbary Coast, Paris, and Bellagio. East on Flamingo are Bourbon Street and Maxim. On the Strip are the Flamingo, O'Shea's, Imperial Palace, Mirage, Harrah's, Casino Royale, the Venetian, and Treasure Island. A leisure traveler could stay a week in this section and not run out of interesting sights, good restaurants, or good entertainment. On the negative side, for those with cars, traffic congestion at the intersection of the Strip and Flamingo Road is the worst in the city.

Strip Cluster 3   Another nice section of the Strip is from Spring Mountain Road to the New Frontier and what was the Desert Inn. The New Frontier can be reached by either of two roads, great for visitors who prefer a major hotel on the Strip but want to avoid the daily traffic snarls. Though the New Frontier is about a quarter mile from the nearest casinos in either direction, it is within a four-minute walk of the excellent Fashion Show Mall. This cluster is a 4-minute cab ride (or 16-minute walk) from the convention center.

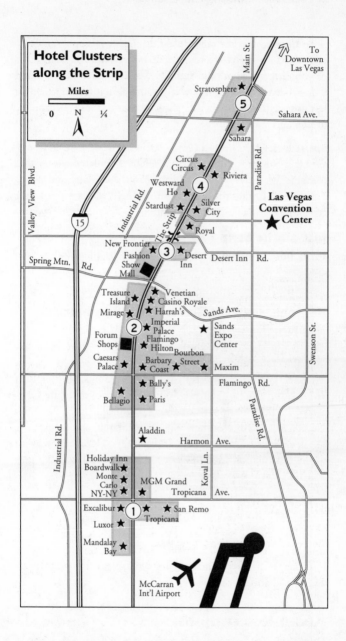

Hotel Clusters along the Strip

Miles

0   N   ¼

To Downtown Las Vegas

Main St.

Stratosphere ★
⑤

Sahara Ave.

Sahara ★

Circus Circus ★
④
Riviera ★

Westward Ho ★

Stardust ★ ★
Silver City ★

Paradise Rd.

Las Vegas Convention Center ★

Royal ★

New Frontier ★
③
Desert Inn ★
Desert Inn Rd.

Fashion Show Mall ■

Spring Mtn. Rd.

Valley View Blvd.

Industrial Rd.

The Strip

15

Treasure Island ★
Venetian ★
Casino Royale ★

Mirage ★
Harrah's ★

②
Imperial Palace ★

Forum Shops ■
Flamingo ★
Hilton ★
Bourbon Street

Caesars Palace ★
Barbary Coast ★
Maxim

Sands Ave.

Sands Expo Center

Swenson St.

Bally's ★

Flamingo Rd.

Bellagio ★
Paris ★

Paradise Rd.

Aladdin ★
Harmon Ave.

Industrial Rd.

Holiday Inn Boardwalk ★
Monte Carlo ★
NY-NY ★

MGM Grand ★ ★
Tropicana

Koval Ln.

Ave.

Excalibur ★
①
Tropicana ★
San Remo ★

Luxor ★

Mandalay Bay ★

McCarran Int'l Airport

33

Strip Cluster 4   The next cluster up the Strip is between Convention Center Drive and Riviera Boulevard. Here, near the convention center, are the Stardust, Westward Ho, Riviera, and Circus Circus. Casinos and hotels in this cluster are considerably less upscale than those in the "grand cluster" but offer acceptable dining and entertainment.

Strip Cluster 5   Finally, near the intersection of Las Vegas Boulevard and Sahara Avenue there is a relatively isolated cluster that contains Wet 'n Wild (a water theme park), the Sahara, and, about a third-mile toward town, the Stratosphere. Visitors with cars are convenient to the Strip, the convention center, and downtown.

Just off the Strip

If you have a car and being on the Strip isn't a big deal to you, excellent hotel-casinos are on Paradise Road and east and west of the Strip on intersecting roads.

Boulder Highway, Green Valley, Summerlin, and North Las Vegas

Twenty minutes from the Strip in North Las Vegas are Texas Station, the Fiesta, and, on the edge of civilization, Santa Fe Station. All have good restaurants, comfortable rooms, and upbeat themes. On the Boulder Highway southeast of town are Castaways, Boulder Station, Sam's Town, Arizona Charlie's East, and Nevada Palace. Also southeast are Sunset Station and the Reserve in Green Valley. These areas cater primarily to locals. Northwest of town is the posh new Regent Las Vegas. Nearby is the new Suncoast Casino.

Sneak Routes

Traffic clogs the heart of the Strip at many hours. Fortunately, most large hotels have back entrances on less-trafficked roads. Industrial Road and I-15 parallel the Strip on the west, providing access to hotels on the west side of Las Vegas Boulevard. Paradise Road and Koval Lane do the same for the east side.

Room Reservations: <u>Getting a Good Room and a Good Deal</u>

Because Las Vegas is popular for short getaways, weekend occupancy averages an astounding 92% of capacity for hotels and

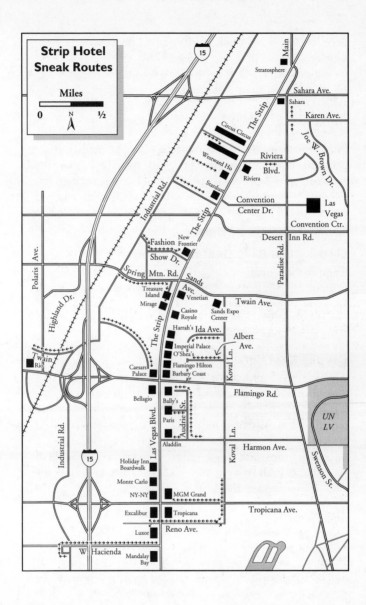

Strip Hotel Sneak Routes

Miles

0   N   ½

15

Stratosphere

Main

Sahara Ave.

Sahara

Karen Ave.

Circus Circus

The Strip

Westward Ho

Riviera Blvd.

Stardust

Riviera

Joe W. Brown Dr.

Convention Center Dr.

Las Vegas Convention Ctr.

Industrial Rd.

The Strip

Desert Inn Rd.

Paradise Rd.

Fashion

New Frontier

Show Dr.

Spring Mtn. Rd.

Sands Ave.

Treasure Island

Venetian

Mirage

Casino Royale

Sands Expo Center

Twain Ave.

Polaris Ave.

Highland Dr.

Harrah's

Ida Ave.

Imperial Palace

O'Shea's

Albert Ave.

Koval Ln.

Twain

Rio

Caesars Palace

Flamingo Hilton

Barbary Coast

Bellagio

Bally's

Flamingo Rd.

UNLV

Las Vegas Blvd.

Paris

Audrie St.

Aladdin

Koval Ln.

Harmon Ave.

Swenson St.

Industrial Rd.

15

Holiday Inn Boardwalk

Monte Carlo

NY-NY

MGM Grand

Excalibur

Tropicana

Tropicana Ave.

Luxor

Reno Ave.

W. Hacienda

Mandalay Bay

35

70% for motels. Weekday occupancy for hotels is a respectable 83%; for motels, 63%. This means: Don't leave home without reservations, especially if major events pack the city.

The Wacky World of Las Vegas Hotel Reservations

Rooms generally are administered by different departments: the casino (for high rollers), the front desk (general public), independent wholesalers (group or individual travel packages), sales and marketing (special events), and national reservations systems. This means the front desk may tell you the hotel is sold out, but a call a few days later may find that rooms unsold by another department are available.

Getting the Best Deal on a Room

Compared to lodging elsewhere, rooms in Las Vegas are so inexpensive that cost-cutting strategies may seem gratuitous. If you are accustomed to paying $120 a night for a room, you can afford 70% of the hotels in town. If, however, you want top value for your dollar, read on.

Beating Rack Rates

The benchmark for making cost comparisons is the hotel's "rack rate," or standard rate. This nondiscounted price is what you would pay if, space available, you walked in off the street and rented a room. Assume that the rack rate is the most you should have to pay.

To learn the standard rate, call room reservations at hotels of your choice. Each type of room will have its own rate. Have the reservationist explain the differences among rooms.

The Season

In December, the town is empty except for National Finals Rodeo week in early December and Christmas/New Year's week. In January, the town is packed during the Consumer Electronics Show and Super Bowl weekend, and pretty much dead otherwise. During these months, most hotels offer amazing deals on lodging. Rates also may be reduced in July and August.

Sorting Out the Sellers and the Options

Given the many sources of rooms, it's almost impossible to find out who is offering the best deal.

Though it's only an approximation, here's a list of rates and packages available, ranked from the best to the worst value.

Room Rates and Packages	Sold or Administered by
1. Gambler's rate	Casino or hotel
2. December, January, and summer specials	Hotel reservations or marketing department
3. Wholesaler packages	Independent wholesalers
4. Tour operator packages	Tour operators
5. Reservation service discounts	Independent wholesalers and consolidators
6. Half-price programs	Half-price program operators
7. Commercial airline packages	Commercial airlines
8. Hotel packages	Hotel sales and marketing
9. Corporate rate	Hotel reservations
10. Hotel standard room rate	Hotel reservations
11. Convention rate	Convention sponsor

Don't forget that if you get the gambler's rate, you'll be obligated to wager, and that could make it the most expensive option.

Taking Advantage of Special Deals

When you call, always ask the reservationist if the hotel has any packages or specials, including gaming specials if you plan to gamble. If the reservationist isn't knowledgeable, ask to be transferred to the sales and marketing staff, and question them.

If you have a lot of time before your trip, contact the hotel and ask about joining its slot club. Although only a few hotels will send you an application, inquiring will categorize you as a gambler on a hotel's mailing list. Once in Las Vegas, join the slot clubs of hotel-casinos you like. This ensures you'll be notified of specials you can use on subsequent visits.

Having shopped the hotel for deals, check tour operator and wholesaler packages advertised in your local newspaper, and compare them with those in the Sunday edition of the *Los Angeles Times*. Next, check packages offered by airline tour services; always ask reservationists if there are specials with any hotels.

Discuss the better deals and packages, regardless of source, with a travel agent. Explain which you favor and ask if he or she can do better. Review all options, then select the deal that best fits your schedule, requirements, and budget.

Timing Is Everything

If occupancy is high for a date, rates will be, too. But if many rooms are available, rates will be lower. This is true all year but especially in "off-peak" times.

At some hotels, a standard room costs 20% less if you check in Monday through Thursday (even though you may stay through the weekend). The rate on the same room with weekend check-in will be higher and may not change if you stay into the following week.

Helping Your Travel Agent to Help You

When you call your travel agent, ask if he or she has been to Las Vegas. Firsthand experience means everything. If the answer is no, find another agent or be prepared to give your agent a lot of direction. Do not accept any recommendations at face value. Check the location and rates of any suggested hotel and make certain it suits your itinerary. Do the same for packages.

Packages in conjunction with airlines, including Delta's Vacations or American's Fly-Away Vacations, will probably be more expensive than those offered by high-volume wholesalers that work with several airlines.

No Room at the Inn (Maybe)   If you're having trouble getting a reservation at the hotel of your choice, let your travel agent assist you. He or she might find a package with a wholesaler or tour operator that bypasses the hotel reservations department. Or, he or she can call the sales and marketing department of the hotel and ask them, as a favor, to find you a room.

No Room at the Inn (for Real)   More frequently than you would imagine, Las Vegas hotels overbook their rooms. To protect yourself, always guarantee your first night with a credit card, send a deposit if required, and insist on a written confirmation of your reservation. Have your confirmation when you check in.

Precautions notwithstanding, the hotel still might have canceled your reservation. If you're told you have no room, demand that the hotel find you a room on the premises or at another convenient hotel (comparable room at the same or better rate). Should the desk clerk balk, demand to see the reservations manager. If the reservations manager stonewalls, go to the general manager. Do not leave until the issue has been resolved.

Where the Deals Are

Tour Operators and Wholesalers

At lower-occupancy days or seasons, hotels allot rooms at considerable discounts to tour operators, travel brokers, travel wholesalers, and travel packagers who resell them for a profit. Sought-after weekend lodging also may be available.

Check the travel section of your Sunday paper for ads for packages or tours to Las Vegas. Book suitable packages directly by calling the phone number listed, or have your travel agent call.

If ads in your paper offer no worthwhile packages, go to a newsstand and buy a Sunday paper, preferably from Los Angeles but also from San Diego, Phoenix, Salt Lake City, Denver, or Chicago. These cities are hot markets for Las Vegas, and their newspapers almost always advertise packages.

Not all of a package may be available to you; air connections may be city-specific. But you may buy the "land only" part of the package. You get the discounted room and amenities (car, shows, etc.) but handle your own travel arrangements.

Half-Price Programs

Most half-price programs charge an annual membership fee or directory subscription charge of $25 to $125. On enrollment, you get a membership card and a directory listing participating hotels. There are many restrictions and exceptions. Also, the discount may be smaller than 50%.

The programs with the largest selection of hotels in Las Vegas are Encore, Travel America at Half Price (Entertainment Publications), International Travel Card, and Quest.

Deeply discounted rooms through half-price programs are not commissionable to travel agents. Thus, you generally must make your own inquiries and reservations.

Half-Price Programs

Encore	(800) 638-0930
Entertainment Publications	(800) 285-5525
International Travel Card	(800) 342-0558
Quest	(800) 638-9819

Players Club

The most visible discount travel club selling Las Vegas is Players Club. The group advertises savings of 25–60% on lodging, cruises, shows, and dining (other destinations are included). Annual membership is $192 (plus $10 handling fee). Participating Las Vegas hotels are Bally's, San Remo, Flamingo Hilton, Las Vegas Hilton, Luxor, Holiday Inn Boardwalk, and Stardust.

A determined person who knows Las Vegas can probably beat Players Club's deal but will have to invest a lot of time for a package only marginally less expensive.

If you're interested in Players Club, call (800) 275-6600. An operator will take your name, address, and phone number. Tell the aggressive telemarketer who calls that you don't have time for the sales pitch, and insist that membership information be mailed to you. Membership cancellation is handled without hassle.

Reservation Services
Wholesalers and consolidators frequently represent themselves as "reservation services." When you call, you can ask for a rate quote for a particular hotel or for their best available deal in a specific area. If there's a maximum you're willing to pay, say so. Chances are, the service will find something that will work for you.

We've found reservation services more useful in finding rooms when they're scarce than in obtaining deep discounts.

Reservation Services

Hotel Reservations Network www.hotelreservationsnetwork.com	(800) 96-HOTEL
Reservations Plus www.resplus.com	(800) 733-6644
RMC Travel Center	(800) 782-2674 or (800) 245-5738
Accommodations Express www.accomodationsexpress.com	(800) 444-7666

Hotel-Sponsored Packages
In addition to selling rooms through tour operators, consolidators, and wholesalers, most hotels periodically offer exceptional deals of their own. Promotion of specials tends to be only in the hotels' primary markets. Look for these specials in Southern California newspapers, or call the hotel. Reservationists usually don't tell you of specials. *You have to ask.*

Exit Information Guide
Exit Information Guide publishes a free book of coupons for bargain rates at hotels throughout California and Nevada. For

$3 ($5 Canadian), EIG will mail a copy (third class) before you make your reservations. Las Vegas properties listed in the guide are generally smaller, nongaming hotels. Contact:

Exit Information Guide
4205 NW Sixth Street
Gainesville, FL 32609
(352) 371-3948
www.roomsaver.com

For Business Travelers

Convention Rates: How the System Works

Business travelers almost always pay more for their rooms than leisure travelers do.

For citywide conventions, huge numbers of rooms are blocked in hotels. Hotels negotiate a rate with the convention sponsor, who then sells the rooms itself. Since hotels prefer gamblers or leisure travelers to conventioneers (who usually have limited time to gamble), the negotiated price tends to be $10–50 per night above rack rate.

Strategies for Beating Convention Rates

To get around convention rates:

1. Buy a package from a tour operator or a wholesaler You won't have to deal with the convention's reservations office or with a hotel's reservations department. Many packages allow you to buy extra days at a discount if the package dates don't coincide with your meeting.

If you beat the convention rate by booking a package or getting a room from a wholesaler, don't blow your cover when you check in. If you walk up to the registration desk in a business suit with a convention badge, the hotel will void your package and charge you the convention rate. Ditto, checkout.

2. Find a hotel that doesn't block rooms Many downtown, North Las Vegas, and Boulder Highway hotels, as well as a few on the Strip, don't block rooms for conventions. Get a list of your convention's "official" hotels and match it against the hotels listed in this guide. Any hotel we list that isn't on the sponsor's list is not blocking rooms for your convention. This means you can deal with the nonparticipating hotels directly and get their regular rate.

3. Reserve late   Thirty to sixty days before a citywide convention or show, the front desk reservations staff in a given hotel will take over management of blocked rooms. "Room Res," in conjunction with the general manager, is responsible for ensuring the hotel runs at capacity during the event. If blocked rooms aren't being booked as expected, the manager may lower the price for attendees. A convention-goer who books a room at the last minute might obtain a rate lower than did attendees who booked early through the sponsor.

The Las Vegas Convention Center

The Las Vegas Convention Center is the nation's largest single-level convention and trade show facility. Almost two million square feet of exhibit space is divided into two main buildings: the brand new South Hall and the older North Hall. A pedestrian bridge over Desert Inn Road connects the halls. In addition to the exhibit areas, the center has a kitchen that can cater a banquet for 12,000 people and 89 meeting rooms. Serving as headquarters for shows and conventions drawing as many as 250,000 delegates, the convention center is on Paradise Road, one very long block off the Strip and three miles from the airport.

The Las Vegas Convention and Visitors Authority also operates Cashman Field Center, home of Las Vegas's AAA baseball team. The center contains a 2,000-seat theater and 100,000 square feet of meeting and exhibit space. For more information, call (702) 892-0711.

Lodging Near the Las Vegas Convention Center

While convention-goers lodge all over town, a few hotels are within walking distance of the convention center.

Next door is the Las Vegas Hilton, with more than 3,100 rooms. The hotel routinely is headquarters for convention center events and offers an additional 220,000 square feet of exhibit, ballroom, banquet, special event, and meeting space. The convention center is a five-minute walk from the Hilton's lobby.

A half-block away (to its rear entrance) is the 2,075-room Riviera Hotel. Like the Hilton, the Riviera is often headquarters for large convention center events and offers supplemental space. The walk from the Riviera's rear (eastern) entrance to the convention center is about ten minutes.

Hotels within a 20-Minute Walk of the Convention Center

Amerisuites	202 suites	7-minute walk
Circus Circus	3,741 rooms	15-minute walk
Las Vegas Courtyard	149 rooms	6-minute walk
Las Vegas Hilton	3,174 rooms	5-minute walk
Mardi Gras Inn	314 suites	12-minute walk
Marriott Suites	255 suites	9-minute walk
New Frontier	988 rooms	20-minute walk
Residence Inn	192 suites	7-minute walk
Riviera	2,075 rooms	10-minute walk
Royal Hotel	220 rooms	12-minute walk
Stardust	2,500 rooms	15-minute walk

Parking at the Las Vegas Convention Center

In all, there are approximately 6,000 parking space in nine color-coded lots. Gold Lots 1–4 make up the bulk of visitor parking; the Gold Lots are located in front of the complex off of Paradise Road. Across Paradise Road from the Gold Lots, between Convention Center Drive and Desert Inn Road, are two Silver Lots. Visitors will want to explore the Gold and Silver lots first.

There are two Orange Lots located off of Desert Inn Road, which runs between the older part of the convention center and the new South Hall expansion. As of press time, parking in the Orange Lots was partially closed off due to construction, with the balance reserved for employees. A single, small Blue Lot located off of Joe W. Brown Drive is currently used by employees and may have little or no space available for conventioneers.

Attendees are often required to enter through the convention center's main entrance. If not parked in the Gold or Silver Lots, convention-goers must hike around the south side of the complex to the front door, a seven- to ten-minute walk. Or, attendees with badges may enter through the doors on the complex's south side.

Cabs and Shuttles to the Convention Center

Citywide conventions often provide complimentary bus service from major hotels. If you are staying at a smaller hotel, walk to the nearest large hotel on the route. Cabs can be scarce at events' daily opening and closing times. City buses ($2) and the Las Vegas Strip Trolley ($1.50) are also available from the larger hotels. Exact fare is required.

Comfort Zones:
Matching Guests with Hotels

Each Las Vegas property targets a carefully defined audience. This effort to please a specific population of guests creates what we call a "comfort zone." If you're in the group a hotel strives to please, you'll feel comfortable and will have much in common with other guests. If you fail to determine the comfort zone before you go, you may choose a hotel you won't enjoy.

Hotel descriptions on subsequent pages detail the atmosphere and clientele of the city's major lodgings.

Democracy in the Casinos

Hotels and casinos continue to be characterized as appealing to "high rollers" (wealthy visitors who gamble in earnest) or "grinds" (less affluent, nickel-and-dime bettors), but the distinction is increasingly blurred. For many years, the slot machine was symbolic of the grinds. Unable to join high-stakes "table games," blue-collar gamblers sat for hours pumping the arms of slots. More recently, however, slot machines' popularity among all gamblers has democratized casinos. The silver-haired lady at the quarter slots is now viewed as a highly valuable customer, and casinos forgo the impression of exclusivity to make her comfortable. After all, slots now contribute 40–100% of a casino's bottom line.

Hotels with Casinos

Aladdin   (www.aladdincasino.com)

With the distinction of being the only strip hotel to be imploded and then rebuilt on the same site, the new Aladdin Resort and Casino is the Las Vegas version of Phoenix rising. The question for the moment, however, is how high can this bird fly? The theme, of course, draws its inspiration from the Arabian Nights tales, which in turn are based on the Islamic culture and folklore of North Africa and the eastern Mediterranean. Dining at the Aladdin is good, with something for every budget.

Arizona Charlie's East and West
(www.azcharlies.com)

Patronized primarily by locals, Arizona Charlie's are working person's casinos with a Southwestern ranch flavor. Everything is informal, and it's busy. The hotel rooms are passable, but the real reason to patronize Arizona Charlie's is the video poker—they're the best machines in town, and considering what town you're in, this means they're among the best machines anywhere.

Bally's (www.ballyslv.com)

A complete resort, Bally's is blessed with exceptional restaurants, one of Las Vegas's better buffets, and *the* best Sunday champagne brunch. Entertainment likewise is top-quality. Guest rooms are large and comfortable, and the hotel is easy to navigate. Bally's caters to meetings and conventions; you will not feel out of place in a business suit. Guests are frequently under age 40, many from Southern California, Chicago, and elsewhere in the Midwest. Bally's also has a loyal Spanish-speaking clientele.

Barbary Coast (www.barbarycoastcasino.com)

The Barbary Coast is an old-fashioned casino for real gamblers. Table games reign supreme. The gourmet restaurant, Michael's, is regarded by many locals as the city's most dependable. There is no showroom or swimming pool, and most rooms are reserved for regular customers.

Bellagio (www.bellagiolasvegas.com)

The Bellagio village is arrayed along the west and north sides of a man-made lake, where dancing fountains provide allure and spectacle. Behind the village facade in a gentle curve is the 3,000-room hotel, complete with casino, restaurants, shopping complex, complete spa, and pool. Imported marble is featured throughout, even in the guest rooms and suites, as are original art, traditionally styled furnishings, and European antiques. Guest rooms and meeting rooms also feature large picture windows affording views of lushly landscaped grounds and formal gardens. Art is everywhere—13 original Picassos, for example, are on exhibit in the restaurant of the same name. Meant to be luxurious, the Bellagio seeks to establish itself as the prestige address of Las Vegas. Room rates have bounced all over the place during Bellagio's first three years and in the future may bounce to a level that you find acceptable.

Boardwalk (www.hiboardwalk.com)

Blessed with a good location next to the Monte Carlo, the Boardwalk is a jumping-off place for guests heading to more imposing surroundings up and down the Strip. Acquired in 1994 by Holiday Inn, the casino was expanded and rebuilt from scratch with a light, airy, Coney Island–boardwalk theme. Though all table games are represented, the emphasis is definitely on slots. Owing to the Holiday Inn connection, guests at the Boardwalk run the gamut.

Boulder Station   (www.boulderstation.com)
Boulder Station is a clone of Palace Station, sharing its railroad theme and emphasis on good food and lounge entertainment. The tasteful casino includes one of the nicest sports books in Las Vegas. Guest rooms in the 300-room hotel tower are modest but comfortable, with good views. Clientele consists primarily of locals and Southern Californians.

Bourbon Street (www.bourbonstreethotel.com)
Bourbon Street is located a block east of the Strip on Flamingo. Known locally as an "overflow" joint, Bourbon Street offers a small casino, a lounge, a coffee shop quality restaurant, and inexpensive guest rooms within easy walking distance of the Strip.

Caesars Palace   (www.caesars.com)
As an exercise in whimsical fantasy and excess, Caesars' Roman theme has been executed with astounding artistry and attention to detail. Gambling at Caesars feels a little like pitching horse-shoes in the Supreme Court, but, incredibly, it works. Caesars Palace provides two spacious and luxurious casinos, excellent restaurants, beautiful landscaping, top celebrity entertainment, exquisite guest rooms, and all of the services and amenities of a world-class resort. The adjoining Forum Shops give Caesars Palace one of the most unique themed shopping complexes in the United States. Caesars is enjoyed by a broad range of clientele from the East, the Midwest, and Southern California.

California   (www.thecal.com)
The California is a pleasant, downtown hotel-casino with excellent, moderately priced restaurants and a largely Hawaiian and Filipino clientele. It is a friendly, mellow place to stay or gamble —unpretentious, but certainly comfortable. The decor is subdued and tasteful, with wood paneling and trim. The shops,

menus, and services work to make visiting Pacific Islanders feel as much at home as visitors from Kansas City or Tampa.

Casino Royale   (www.casinoroyalehotel.com)

Located across the Strip from the Mirage, the diminutive Casino Royale has about 150 guest rooms. Small, accessible, and unpretentious, Casino Royale provides bargain lodging in the Strip's high-rent district. The property's clientele runs the gamut from tour groups to convention-goers on a tight budget to folks who could not get rooms at other hotels on the block.

Castaways   (www.showboat-lv.com)

Castaways, formerly the Showboat, is on Boulder Highway not far from downtown. A 100-lane bowling alley gives this property its informal, sporty identity. The casino, busy but not overcrowded, includes an immense bingo parlor. Restaurants offer a good value for the dollar. There is also good lounge entertainment.

Circus Circus   (www.circuscircus.com)

Children, young adults, retirees, and the novice (or modest) gambler are welcome here. The labyrinthine casino has low ceilings and is frenetic, loud, and always busy. Circus Circus has a very good steak house (the only escape from the circus theme); a huge, inexpensive buffet; an RV park; and a monorail shuttle that connects the property's two main buildings. In 1993, Circus Circus launched what is now the Adventuredome, a desert canyon– themed amusement park totally enclosed in a giant pink dome. In 1997 Circus Circus opened a new hotel tower as well as a shopping and restaurant arcade adjoining Adventuredome.

Desert Inn   (www.thedesertinn.com)

Steve Wynn, after selling the Mirage, Golden Nugget, and Bellagio, purchased the Desert Inn. Within three months he closed the venerable casino and is currently in the process of replacing the DI with a new 2,600-room resort.

El Cortez   (www.elcortez.net)

El Cortez, east of downtown, caters to seniors, motor coach tours, and blue-collar locals. The rambling casino is congested; slots are the major draw. Food and drink are bargains, and loose slots give a lot of play for patrons' money. While guest rooms at

El Cortez have not been recently renovated, they're quite nice and an exceptional value.

Excalibur   (www.excaliburcasino.com)

By combining a Knights of the Round Table theme, restaurants with giant portions, family-oriented entertainment, and moderate costs, the Excalibur "packs 'em in," especially on weekends. A Las Vegas rendition of a medieval realm, the Excalibur is oversized, garish, and more in the image of Kmart than of King Arthur. The Excalibur is the third-largest hotel in the United States, and it certainly features the world's largest hotel parking lot (so far removed from the entrance that trams are dispatched to haul in the patrons). If you can get past the fact that most guest rooms have showers only (no tubs), and you do not object to joining the masses, there is good value to be had at the Excalibur.

Fiesta   (www.fiestacasinohotel.com)

The Mexican-themed Fiesta was the first of several casinos at the intersection of Rancho Drive and Lake Mead Boulevard in North Las Vegas. It has 100 guest rooms, a slot-packed casino, a food court, and a country dance hall. Mexican and southwestern restaurants are the major draw. On Sunday is a good Margarita Brunch. The Fiesta draws locals.

Fitzgeralds   (www.fitzgeralds.com)

Located downtown, Fitzgeralds' casino is large and compartmentalized with gold press-metal ceilings, mirrored columns, and print carpet with little Irish hats. Rooms on the upper floors of the Fitz afford some of the best views in town, and corner rooms with hot tubs are a great bargain. Guests tend to be older travelers and retirees from the Midwest. In the casino, the crowd is a mixed bag of regulars and bargain hunters.

Flamingo   (www.flamingolv.com)

The first super-resort on the Strip, the Flamingo's 3,642 rooms, four towers, and prime location, is the centerpiece of the Strip's most prestigious block. A Hilton property, the Flamingo offers an ambience comfortable to leisure and business travelers alike. The large, bustling casino retains the bright Miami pinks, magentas, and tangerines that established the Flamingo's identity more than four decades ago, but the hotel lobby, rooms, and services are standard Hilton. The hotel's clientele comes in all colors and sizes, and from all over the country (but especially Southern California). The Flamingo actively cultivates the Japanese market and also does a strong business with tour wholesalers.

Four Queens   (www.fourqueens.com)

The Four Queens downtown offers good food, renovated guest rooms, and a positively cheery casino. Glistening, light decor enhanced by tropical-print carpet makes the casino feel fun, upbeat, and clean. Hotel guests tend to be middle-aged or older and come from Southern California, Texas, Hawaii, and the Midwest. Locals love Hugo's Cellar restaurant.

Four Seasons (www.fourseasons.com/lasvegas)

The Four Seasons is an exclusive, 400-room, noncasino hotel contained by the greater Mandalay Bay megaresort. The lobby area has a plush feel, decorated with wood, Victorian sofas and easy chairs, a grand piano, and even a fireplace. Four Seasons' rooms are on the 35th–39th floors of the Mandalay Bay tower. Private express elevators deliver guests to the Four Seasons' floors. Rates come at a hefty premium over Mandalay Bay's rooms, which are nearly identical. Four Seasons will appeal to ultra-upscale travelers looking for a mini-oasis that insulates them from the hullabaloo of Las Vegas. But it doesn't come cheap.

Fremont   (www.fremontcasino.com)

Sam Boyd's Fremont is a downtown landmark. It offers good food, budget lodging, and a robust, crowded casino. Table games are played beneath a high ceiling ringed in neon; slots cram narrow aisles. Locals, Asians, Hawaiians, and Southern Californians love the Fremont.

Frontier, The New   (www.frontierlv.com)

The Frontier has been through the wringer . . . oops, make that the *New* Frontier. This is the hotel that essentially launched Siegfried & Roy in Las Vegas, the hotel with a super location smack in the middle of the Strip, and the hotel with owners who allowed it to get embroiled in a labor dispute and strike that lasted six and a half years. In 1998, Phil Ruffin bought the Frontier, quickly settled the strike, and christened the property the New Frontier. Since then, Ruffin has poured millions of dollars into repairs and improvements. The renovated guest rooms, new Chinese and Italian restaurants, and Gilley's Saloon stand out proudly. The New Frontier is staging a remarkable comeback. It is easily accessed from Fashion Show Drive or the Strip and is within easy walking distance of some of the best shopping in town.

Gold Coast   (www.goldcoastcasino.com)
The Gold Coast, a half mile west of the Strip, is a local's hangout. A casual inspection reveals nothing unique: The Gold Coast provides lounge entertainment at all hours, offers headliners and modest production shows in its showroom, and makes sure it has the locals' favorite slots. There is also a two-screen movie complex and a huge bowling alley. Free transportation is provided to the casino's sister property, the Barbary Coast.

Gold Spike   (www.goldspikehotelcasino.com)
About a four-minute walk from Fremont Street, the Gold Spike is basically a slot joint. It's congested and loud, luring customers with low minimums, cheap food, and $20 rooms.

Golden Gate   (www.goldengatecasino.net)
Devoted primarily to slots, the downtown Golden Gate is crowded and dingy but redeems itself by offering one of the city's best shrimp cocktail specials. The hotel has 106 budget rooms.

Golden Nugget   (www.goldennugget.com)
The undisputed flagship of the downtown hotels, the Golden Nugget is smack in the middle of Glitter Gulch. The hotel offers bright, cheery rooms with tropical decor, a first-rate showroom, lounge entertainment, excellent restaurants, a large pool, a top-notch spa, a shopping arcade, and a workout room. The casino is clean and breezy. The feel here is definitely upscale, though comfortable and informal. The Golden Nugget attracts people from New York, Dallas, Chicago, Los Angeles, and San Diego, as well as visitors from Taiwan, Hong Kong, and Japan. Younger travelers (ages 28–39) like the Golden Nugget, as do older tourists.

Green Valley Ranch Station
The newest of the Station casinos, Green Valley Ranch Station is located about 15 minutes east of the Strip in an upscale residential area. The property offers a 200-room hotel, a casino with

40 table games and almost 2,500 slot and video poker machines, 6 restaurants including a buffet, a spa, and a 10-screen cinema complex. Like all Station casinos, Green Valley Ranch Station provides locals with high-pay slots, good dining value, an excellent slot club, and high quality lounge entertainment.

Hard Rock Hotel (www.hardrockhotel.com)

The Hard Rock is billed as the world's first rock-and-roll hotel and casino. Like the adjoining Hard Rock Cafe, it's loaded with rock memorabilia. Everywhere it's rock, rock, rock, from lounge music to piano-shaped roulette tables. Surprisingly tasteful guest rooms offer nice views. The Joint is Las Vegas's most intimate live-rock venue. Hard Rock targets baby boomers, younger Southern Californians, midwesterners, and urban northeasterners.

Harrah's Las Vegas (www.harrahslasvegas.com)

Unpretentious and upbeat, Harrah's offers tasteful guest rooms as well as a beautiful showroom, a comedy club, above-average restaurants and buffet, a pool, an exercise room, and a spa. The L-shaped casino is bright and roomy and the mood is light-hearted. Its clientele tends to be older midwesterners and Southern Californians, and business and convention travelers. Other features include a renovated swimming area, a new bar/restaurant with an outdoor patio, a steak house with a view of the Strip, and Carnival Court, an outdoor plaza with fountains and street entertainment.

Horseshoe (www.binions.com)

Binion's Horseshoe is an anchor in Glitter Gulch. The casino is large and active, with row upon row of slots clanking under a suffocatingly low ceiling. Table games are less congested. Old West–themed, the Horseshoe is one of the city's top spots for poker and craps. There's no maximum on wagers; bet a million if you wish. Locals and "real gamblers" hang out here.

Imperial Palace (www.imperial-palace.com)

The Imperial Palace has a large, active casino lavishly executed with mammoth chandeliers and carved beams. There is a lovely swimming and sunbathing area complete with waterfall, and a Nautilus-equipped exercise room and spa. *Legends in Concert,* one of the hottest shows in Las Vegas, plays nightly at the Imperial Palace's showroom. Most of the guest rooms at the Imperial Palace are modern and of Holiday Inn–level quality.

Lady Luck (www.ladyluck.com)

The Lady Luck downtown offers nice rooms (or small suites) at a great price, an excellent restaurant (the Burgundy Room), and a large, uncomplicated casino. Clientele includes Filipinos, Asian Americans, Californians, motor coach tourists, and locals.

Las Vegas Club (www.playatlvc.com)

The Las Vegas Club is a downtown hotel-casino with a sports theme. The casino is modest and has some of the more player-friendly blackjack rules around. Request a room in the North Tower. The property draws Hawaiians, midwesterners, bus groups, and seniors.

Las Vegas Hilton (www.lv-hilton.com)

Next door to the Las Vegas Convention Center, the Hilton does more meeting, trade show, and convention business than any other hotel in town. A 10- to 12-minute walk from the Strip, the Hilton operates under the valid assumption that many of its guests leave the hotel only to go to the convention center. The Las Vegas Hilton has some of the best restaurants in town. In 1998, the Hilton premiered *Star Trek: The Experience,* an interactive video and virtual reality amusement center featuring a space-flight simulation ride. The casino, like the hotel itself, is huge and tastefully businesslike. If you can afford it, the Hilton is the most convenient place to stay in town if you are attending a trade show or convention at the Las Vegas Convention Center. If, however, you are in Las Vegas for pleasure, staying at the Hilton is like being in luxurious exile.

Luxor (www.luxor.com)

Rising 30 stories, the Luxor is a huge pyramid with guest rooms situated around the outside perimeter from base to apex. Guest room hallways circumscribe a hollow core containing the world's largest atrium. Inside the atrium, inclinators rise at a 39° angle from the pyramid's corners to access the guest floors. Open and attractive, the 100,000-square-foot casino is tasteful by any standard. Inside you'll find an attraction designed by Douglas

Trumbull, creator of the *Back to the Future* ride at Universal Studios Florida, and an IMAX theater. In addition to the attractions, three restaurants, a huge electronic games arcade, and a collection of retail shops are on this level. Decorated in an understated Egyptian motif, the standard guest rooms are large and among the most nicely appointed in town. The only disappointment is that many of the 4,474 guest rooms do not have tubs.

Main Street Station (www.mainstreetcasino.com)

Main Street Station downtown accommodates overflow guests from the California across the street. The casino echoes a turn-of-the-last-century gentleman's club and contains enough antiques and art to furnish a museum. With refurbished guest rooms, a brew pub, and an excellent buffet, the property is interesting and fun.

Mandalay Bay   (www.mandalaybay.com)

Circus Circus's Mandalay Bay opened in spring 1999 on the old Hacienda site. It's a megaresort in the true sense of the overworked word—3,700 guest rooms rank it as the fifth-largest hotel in Las Vegas. Mandalay Bay is a Burmese-themed clone of the Mirage, Treasure Island, and Bellagio. The sprawling complex features the 43-story, three-wing tower; an arena; a theater; a concert venue; a dozen restaurants; a water park; three large lounges; and the 400-room Four Seasons hotel. The signature spectacle is the four-story wine tower at Aureole. Mandalay Bay appeals to a young, hip, fun-seeking, upscale market. All the different ideas jammed into Mandalay Bay might not always add up to a cohesive whole, but so many parts of the sum are unique that it makes for an interesting series of sights.

MGM Grand Hotel and Casino (www.mgmgrand.com)

At the MGM Grand, the evolutionary combination of gambling resort and attraction was carried to the next logical stage, the development of a theme park on an equal footing with the casino. As it happened, however, the theme park was highly publicized but pitifully designed. In 2000, after seven years of limping along, the MGM (not so) Grand Adventures park closed.

It claims the distinction of being both the largest hotel in the United States (with 5,036 rooms) and the world's largest casino. There are two showrooms at the MGM Grand. In addition, its special-events arena can accommodate boxing, tournament tennis, rodeo, and basketball, as well as major exhibitions. Amenities at the MGM Grand, not unexpectedly, are among the best in Las Vegas. The swimming complex is huge—23,000 square feet of pool area, with 5 interconnected pools graced with bridges, fountains, and waterfalls. The newest addition to the entertainment mix is Lion Habitat, where you can watch live lions. A first at the MGM Grand is a youth center that provides supervised programs for children (ages 3–12) of hotel guests both day and night.

The MGM Grand's biggest problem, weekend hotel registration and check-out, has been addressed with a registration desk at the airport where guests can check in and pick up room keys while waiting for their baggage.

The MGM Grand derives 80% of its business from individual travelers and tour and travel groups, with only 10% coming from trade show and convention attendees. The youth center and PG-rated showroom entertainment make the MGM Grand a natural for families. Room rates in the $90–140 range make the MGM Grand accessible to a broad population.

Mirage   (www.themirage.com)

Exciting and compelling without being whimsical or silly, the Mirage blends the stateliness of marble with the exotic luxury of tropical greenery and polished bamboo. Casino, showroom, shopping, restaurants, and lounges are artfully integrated.

Outside, instead of blinking neon, the Mirage has a 55-foot-tall erupting volcano that disrupts traffic on the Strip every half hour. The restaurants at the Mirage are special, especially Kokomo's, with its seafood specialties. Illusionists Siegfried and Roy are the headliners in one of two showrooms. Impressionist Danny Gans performs in the other. Amenities include a stunning swimming complex and stylish shopping arcade. The magnificent casino is huge yet informal. Guest rooms are among the city's nicest.

Although guests pay top dollar, the hotel remains one of Clark County's top tourist attractions. Whether by foot, bus, trolley, cab, or bicycle, every Las Vegas visitor makes at least one pilgrimage.

Monte Carlo   (www.monte-carlo.com)

Its 3,002 guest rooms rank Monte Carlo as Las Vegas's seventh-largest hotel and the world's eighth-largest. It's modeled after the Place du Casino in Monte Carlo, Monaco, with ornate arches, fountains, and marble floors.

Guest rooms, with marble entryways and French period art, are mid- to upper-priced to compete with the MGM Grand. Amenities include a swimming complex with slides, wave pool, and float stream; an exceptional fitness center; an interesting shopping arcade; and a brew pub with live entertainment. The football-field-sized casino has simulated skylights and domes. The showroom is designed for illusionist Lance Burton.

Compared to the powerful settings of New York–New York, Treasure Island, and Luxor, the Monte Carlo's turn-of-the-last-century theme doesn't generate much excitement. But, Monte Carlo is an attractive hotel-casino rather than a crowded tourist attraction.

New York–New York
(www.nynyhotelcasino.com)

Although small by megaresort standards ("only" about 2,000 rooms), New York–New York triumphs in the realization of its theme. Guest rooms are in towers reminiscent of the Big Apple skyline, including the Empire State, Chrysler, and Seagrams buildings. The buildings are connected, but each offers different decor and ambience.

A half-sized Statue of Liberty and a replica of Grand Central Station lead visitors to one entrance, while the Brooklyn Bridge beckons to another. The property's interior is divided into themed areas, including Greenwich Village, Wall Street, and Times Square. The casino looks like a movie set. Table games and slots are sandwiched between buildings, shops, restaurants, and well-executed city street facades.

Like its namesake, New York–New York is extremely congested and always awash with sightseers. Aisles and indoor paths are far too narrow to accommodate the crowds, and New York–New York succumbs periodically to pedestrian gridlock.

If you long for the thrill of a Big Apple cab ride, hop on the roller coaster. It's the fourth on the Strip but the only one where people on the street can hear riders scream. Our favorite New York–New York feature is Hamilton's, a cozy piano bar overlooking the casino.

Guest rooms approximate the Holiday Inn standard but are disappointing for a hotel with such a strong theme. Likewise, the swimming area and fitness center are only average. Full-service restaurants are above average and fast food quite interesting.

Nevada Palace   (www.nvpalace.com)

The Nevada Palace is a small Boulder Highway property patronized primarily by locals and by seniors who take advantage of its 168-space RV park. Pleasant, the Nevada Palace is a friendly, less hectic alternative to staying downtown or on the Strip.

Orleans   (www.orleanscasino.com)

The 840-room Orleans, marketed primarily to locals, has a New Orleans/bayou theme executed in a cavernous building. The festive casino includes a two-story replication of a French Quarter street and a couple of nifty bars. Restaurants have little to do with the Louisiana theme. Upstairs is a 70-lane bowling complex. Recent additions include a movie complex and childcare center.

Palace Station   (www.palacestation.com)

Palace Station is a local favorite that's beginning to attract tourists. With a top buffet, restaurants (crowded) offering amazing specials, a tower of handsome guest rooms, good prices, and access to downtown and the Strip, Palace Station has arrived. The railroad-themed casino is large and busy. Slots are reportedly loose. Lounge entertainment is first-rate.

The Palms   (www.thepalmslasvegas.com)

Located west of the Strip, Palms opened in late 2001. Though it primarily targets a youthful local market, Palms offers the amenities of many Strip casinos, including a roomy 95,000-square-foot casino, a 42-story hotel tower, several entertainment venues, and a 14-screen cinema. Key is a central pool complex that will be a magnet for hip, younger guests. A bar on top of the hotel tower, six restaurants, plus a possible top-ten contender buffet round out the batting order.

Paris Las Vegas   (www.paris-lv.com)

Paris echoes its namesake, with a 50-story Eiffel Tower (with restaurant atop), an Arc de Triomphe, and a River Seine with boat rides. Thrown in for good measure are the Champs-Elysées, Parc Monceau, and Paris Opera House. Opened in September 1999, Paris offers 13 restaurants, shopping, a 25,000-square-foot spa, and an 85,000-square-foot casino.

Plaza   (www.plazahotelcasino.com)

The Plaza is the only Las Vegas hotel with its own railroad station. Not long ago, the hotel was run-down, but tower rooms were renovated and are now available at very good prices. It's the only downtown hotel offering tennis and one of only two with showrooms. The restaurant looks straight down Glitter Gulch and the Fremont Experience; reserve a window table.

The table gaming area is very pleasant. Patrons include walk-ins, attendees of small meetings, and Southern Californians.

Quality Inn and Key Largo Casino (www.keylargocasino.com)

Though small, it has all the essentials (mini-casino, restaurant, gift shop, lounge, pool). The Quality's crowning glory is a green and extraordinarily peaceful central courtyard and pool complex. Its location permits easy access to the Strip and the airport.

Regent Las Vegas   (www.regentlasvegas.com)

The Regent Las Vegas offers a Scottsdale/Palm Beach resort experience as an alternative to the madness of the Strip. Near Red Rock Canyon, the Regent Las Vegas consists of two southwestern-style hotels built around the TPC golf course. The resort offers a classy, comfortable casino with 1,200 slots and 40 table games, an 11-acre garden, and a large swimming complex. While guest rooms are spacious and among the nicest in Las Vegas, the real draw here is the golf and the spa. The core market is locals.

Reserve   (www.vegas.com/resorts/reserve)

The Reserve, targeting locals, is a safari-themed hotel-casino southeast of Las Vegas. Although the theme is well executed, many people are reminded of a Rainforest Cafe with gambling. Available are a 42,000-square-foot casino, a popular lounge, a good buffet, several restaurants (try the steakhouse), and adequate guest rooms. In 2000, the Reserve was acquired by Station casinos.

Rio   (www.playrio.com)

The Rio is one of Las Vegas's treasures and our first choice for romantic getaways or honeymoons. Tastefully decorated in a Latin American carnival theme, it's a true destination resort. Rooms (all plush suites) offer exceptional views and cost the same as regular rooms at many other hotels. The Rio has excellent restaurants, a great buffet, high-energy entertainment, a huge shopping arcade, and an elaborate swimming area. The casino includes a comfortable sports book. Masquerade Village shopping venue, which surrounds the casino, offers "Masquerade in the Sky," a parade featuring floats and performers suspended from tracks high above the casino floor. The Rio draws both locals and out-of-towners, particularly Southern Californians.

Riviera   (www.theriviera.com)

Extending from the Strip halfway to the Las Vegas Convention Center, the Riviera accommodates both leisure and business travelers. It offers so much that many guests never leave the property. It has more long-running shows (four) than any other Las Vegas hotel and offers unusually varied entertainment, including production, striptease, female impersonator, and celebrity shows.

Some hotels serve better food, but few offer more variety, especially to the informal diner, who can choose among fast-food restaurants and the buffet. Amenities include a wedding chapel. Guest rooms, particularly in the towers, are surprisingly comfortable.

The huge casino is something of a maze. There's always noise, light, and activity. Walk-in traffic mixes with convention-goers, retirees on "gambling sprees," Asians, Asian Americans, and Southern Californians.

Sahara   (www.saharahotelandcasino.com)

A complex of buildings and towers, the Sahara offers a casino, a convention hall, a showroom, a decent buffet, a shopping arcade, two upscale restaurants, and a swimming pool. Fronting the building along the Strip are two attractions worth noting: Speedworld, a virtual reality racecar "ride"; and Speed, a roller coaster.

The Sahara is comfortable but not flashy. Guest rooms are modern, and the new casino, with its Moroccan styling, is both tasteful and visually exciting. Conventioneers, Southern Californians, and southwesterners predominate among patrons.

Sam's Town   (www.samstownlv.com)

Sam's Town is a rambling property with an Old West mining-town motif. In addition to the hotel and casino are a bowling alley, a very good buffet, one of Las Vegas's better Mexican eateries, a steakhouse, a great 1950s-style diner, and two RV parks. The lounge features live country-western music and dancing and is popular with both locals and visitors. A new events center and an 18-screen movie theater were added in 2000. Frequent customers, besides the locals, include seniors and cowboys.

San Remo   (www.sanremolasvegas.com)

The San Remo, across from the MGM Grand, traditionally attracts business travelers, Southern Californians, southwesterners, and the Japanese.

It has a chandeliered casino, an OK restaurant, an average buffet, a great prime rib special, and a good sushi bar. Guest rooms are well appointed.

Santa Fe Station   (www.stationsantafe.com)

Santa Fe Station targets both locals and tourists. Acquired by Station Casinos in 2000, the name was changed from Santa Fe to Santa Fe Station. Bright and airy with a warm southwestern decor, Santa Fe Station is one of the more livable hotel-casinos. It offers a spacious casino, a better-than-average buffet, and an all-purpose restaurant. Live entertainment is provided in the lounge. In addition to a pool, there is a bowling alley and, amazingly, a hockey-sized ice-skating rink.

Silverton   (www.silvertoncasino.com)

The casino is visually interesting, with rough-hewn beams, mine tunnels, overhead mine car tracks, and a sizable array of prospecting and mining artifacts. The buffet and coffee shop are better than average. The lounge features country music and dancing. Silverton targets Southern Californians and the RV crowd with a large, full-service RV park.

Stardust   (www.stardustlv.com)

The Stardust is well placed for Strip action and is about a 15-minute walk from the Las Vegas Convention Center. A high-rise tower, amenities include a shopping arcade and a heated pool. The Stardust has consistent, high-quality restaurants such as William B's, which features some of Las Vegas's better prime rib.

Wayne Newton signed a contract with the Stardust guaranteeing he will perform his show here exclusively. The casino was renovated to the tune of $24 million in 1999.

Stratosphere   (www.stratlv.com)

The 1,149-foot-tall Stratosphere Tower is the tallest building west of the Mississippi—taller than the Eiffel Tower (the real one). It houses indoor and outdoor observation decks, a revolving restaurant, four wedding chapels, and meeting rooms. The 360° view is breathtaking day and night. A hotel-casino is adjacent. At the top of the tower are two thrill rides. The world's highest roller coaster is also the world's slowest and shortest. The other ride, however, called the Big Shot, is a monster: it rockets riders up the tower's needle with a force of four g's, then drops them back with no g's. And it all happens 1,000 feet in the air! A second construction phase, including another 1,000 rooms and a new pool area, was completed in 2001.

Suncoast   (www.suncoastcasino.com)

Like most of the Coast casinos, Suncoast is designed to attract locals. Located west of Las Vegas in Summerlin near some of the area's best golf courses, Suncoast offers high-return slots and video poker, a fitness center, bowling, and a 16-screen movie complex. There's a decent buffet and restaurants serving Italian, Mexican, and big wads of meat respectively. The southwestern, mission-style casino is open and uncrowded. A showroom that features name bands, a new pool, and a childcare center round out the offerings.

Terrible's
(www.terribleherbst.com/ett-gaming/casino-hotel)

Located a couple of blocks off the Strip at the intersection of Paradise and Flamingo Roads, Terrible's offers excellent value with totally refurbished guest rooms, a good buffet, and a casino that's clean, bright, and busy. Terrible, incidently, is a person, Terrible

Herbst to be exact. Terrible's targets locals but is a good choice, by virtue of its location and easy parking, for anyone who has a car and intends to use it.

Texas Station   (www.texasstation.com)

Texas Station has a single-story full-service casino with 91,000 square feet of gaming space; the atmosphere is contemporary western. This property offers seven restaurants, one of Las Vegas's best buffets, two bars, a dance hall, a bowling center, childcare, and a 12-screen theater. Texas Station caters to locals and cowboys. It's at the intersection of Rancho Drive and Lake Mead Boulevard in North Las Vegas.

Treasure Island   (www.treasureisland.com)

Like the Mirage next door, Treasure Island is both hotel-casino and attraction, but it targets a younger, more middle-class family clientele. Visitors entering the hotel from the Strip cross Buccaneer Bay on a plank bridge and transit a Caribbean pirate fort landscaped with palms. Through the main sally port is the commercial and residential area of Buccaneer Bay Village, complete with town square, shops, restaurants, and, of course, casino. To the usual slots and table games is added a comfortable sports book. Pirate's Walk, the main interior passageway, leads to a shopping arcade, steakhouse, and buffet. The upscale Buccaneer Bay Club restaurant overlooks the sea battle.

Treasure Island is home to the extraordinary *Cirque du Soleil,* which performs in a custom-designed, 1,500-seat theater. Mutiny Bay is an electronic-games arcade for kids.

Tropicana   (www.tropicanalv.com)

With its Paradise and Island Towers and 1,910 rooms, the Tropicana offers a full range of services and amenities. It's also home to one of Las Vegas's most celebrated swimming complexes. The bustling and bright casino ranks as one of the city's more pleasant and exciting places to gamble. Casino clientele is younger than average and includes guests from Excalibur enjoying the Trop's more sophisticated style. It's particularly popular with slot players. The guest rooms' tropical motif is exotic and in some cases includes mirrored ceilings. Views from the towers' upper rooms are among the city's best. The Tropicana targets wholesalers, bus tours, and the Japanese and Hispanic markets. Southern Californians abound.

Vacation Village (www.vacationvillage.com)

The most remote property at the south end of the Strip, Vacation Village provides budget lodging and basic amenities. Guests find a nice southwestern-decor casino, pool, buffet, and Mexican restaurant. The property is friendly and welcomes families, but its isolation is a drawback.

The Venetian (www.venetian.com)

Visiting the Venetian is like taking a trip back to the artistic, architectural, and commercial center of the world in the sixteenth century. You cross a 585,000-gallon canal on the steep-pitched Rialto Bridge, shadowed by the Campanile Bell Tower, to enter the Doge's Palace. Characters in period costumes from the twelfth to seventeenth centuries roam the public areas singing opera, performing mime, and jesting.

Although the Venetian claims that its bread and butter customers are business travelers and shoppers, it hasn't neglected to include a casino in its product mix. When the Lido Casino comes on line with the completion of Phase II, the overall resort will top out at more than 200,000 square feet of casino, second only to the MGM Grand. Upstairs is the Grand Canal Shoppes with 65 stores, mostly small boutiques. The centerpiece of the mall is the quarter-mile Grand Canal itself. Gondolas ply the waterway, steered and powered by gondoliers who serenade the four passengers in each ($10 adults, $5 children).The Venetian's 16 restaurants, most designed by well-known chefs, provide a wide range of dining environments and culinary choice.

An all-suite hotel, the development plan calls for two Y-shaped hotel towers, each with 3,000 suites connected directly to the Sands Expo and Convention Center. The five-pool swimming complex and spa area are situated on the roof-top over the shopping venue and are well insulated from the bustle of the Strip.

The Venetian targets the convention market with its mix of high-end business lodging, power restaurants, unique shopping, and proximity to Sands Expo and Convention Center. The Venetian will certainly welcome tourists and gamblers, who come mostly on the weekend, but the other five days will be monopolized by the trade show crowds.

Westward Ho   (www.westwardho.com)

A sprawling motel next to the Stardust, the Westward Ho offers a slot-oriented casino decorated in the usual dark colors. There are lounge entertainment, a couple of pools, palatable dining, good deals on drinks and snacks, and easy access to nearby casinos.

Suite Hotels

Suites

The term *suite* means many things in Las Vegas. Most suites are larger-than-average rooms with a conversation area (couch, chair, and coffee table) and a refrigerator. In a two-room suite, conversation and sleeping areas normally are separate. Two-room suites are not necessarily larger than one-room suites but are more versatile. One- and two-room suites cost about the same as a standard room.

Only the Rio and Venetian are all-suite properties.

A number of suite hotels don't have casinos. Patronized primarily by business travelers and nongamblers, they offer a quiet alternative to frenetic casino hotels. But because there's no gambling to subsidize operations, suites usually cost more at non-casino hotels.

Suite Hotels without Casinos

AmeriSuites   (www.amerisuites.com)

AmeriSuites offers tidy, one-room suites at good prices. In addition to a small fitness center, an outdoor pool, and a few small meeting rooms, the AmeriSuites serves complimentary continental breakfast. By taxi, AmeriSuites is four minutes from the Strip and five minutes from the Las Vegas Convention Center.

Alexis Park   (www.alexispark.com)

This is the best known of Las Vegas's one- and two-room suite properties. Expensive and relatively exclusive, it offers most of the amenities of a large resort. Suites are upscale and plush, with southwestern decor. Staff is friendly and unpretentious. The Alexis Park has filed a request to add a small casino; if this is a turn-off, call before you go. Guests include executive business travelers and Southern California yuppies.

Crowne Plaza Holiday Inn (www.crowneplaza.com)

Suites are mostly of the two-room variety and are nicely, but not luxuriously, appointed. There is a pool and a cafe, and a fine selection of ethnic restaurants are within easy striking distance.

Holiday Inn Emerald Springs (www.holidayinnlasvegas.com)

The pink stucco Holiday Inn offers moderately priced one- and two-room suites, plus a lounge, pool, and spa. Public areas and rooms are tranquil and sedate. The Veranda Cafe serves a breakfast buffet.

Mardi Gras Inn Best Western (www.bestwestern.com)

The Mardi Gras offers Spartan suites at good rates. Quiet, with a well-manicured courtyard and pool, it's a short walk from the convention center. A coffee shop is on site. The "casino" is only a few slot machines.

Marriott Suites   (www.marriott.com)

Amenities are plentiful: outdoor pool and hot tub, fitness center, full-service restaurant, and room service. The small building is easy to navigate, and parking is convenient. Suites are tasteful.

Residence Inn   (www.residenceinn.com)

Across from the convention center, the Residence Inn by Marriott offers comfortable one- and two-bedroom suites with full kitchens and is more homelike than other suite properties. Amenities include a coin laundry.

St. Tropez   (www.sttropezlasvegas.com)

The St. Tropez offers beautifully decorated one- and two-room suites, often at less than $100 per night. Adjoining a small mall, St. Tropez provides a restaurant, lounge, pool, fitness center, VCRs in suites, and complimentary buffet breakfast. Most guests are upscale business travelers.

Las Vegas Motels

Because they compete with the huge hotel-casinos, many Las Vegas motels offer great rates or provide special amenities, including complimentary breakfast. National motel chains are well represented. We included some motels in the ratings and rankings section to indicate how these properties compare with hotel-casinos and all-suite hotels.

Hotel-Casinos and Motels: Rated and Ranked

Room Ratings

To separate properties according to the relative quality, tastefulness, state of repair, cleanliness, and size of standard room, we have grouped the hotels and motels in classifications denoted by stars. Our star ratings apply to Las Vegas properties only and don't necessarily correspond to ratings awarded by Mobil, AAA, or other travel critics.

Star ratings apply to room quality only and describe the property's standard accommodations: for most, a hotel room with either one king bed or two queen beds. In an all-suite property, the standard accommodation is either a one- or two-room suite. Amenities and location aren't factors in our ratings.

In addition to stars (which delineate broad categories), we also use a numerical rating system. Our rating scale is 0–100, with 100 as the best possible rating. Numerical ratings are presented to show the difference we perceive between one property and another.

ROOM STAR RATINGS

★★★★★	Superior Rooms	Tasteful and luxurious by any standard
★★★★	Extremely Nice Rooms	What you would expect at a Hyatt Regency or Marriott
★★★	Nice Rooms	Holiday Inn or comparable quality
★★	Adequate Rooms	Clean, comfortable, and functional, without frills—like a Motel 6
★	Super Budget	

How the Hotels Compare

In most hotels, the better rooms are in high-rise "towers." The more modest "garden rooms" are found in one- and two-story outbuildings.

Because we can't check every room in a hotel, we inspect several randomly chosen rooms and base our rating on those. Inspections are conducted anonymously and without management's knowledge. It's possible that the rooms we inspect are representative but that by bad luck a guest is assigned an inferior room.

To avoid disappointment, investigate in advance. When you make inquiries, obtain a photo of a hotel's standard room or a promotional brochure before you book. (Note: Some chains use the same guest room photo in their promotional literature for all hotels in the chain.) Ask how old the property is and when your room was last renovated. If you arrive and are assigned an inferior room, demand to be moved.

Cost estimates are based on the hotel's published rack rates for standard rooms, averaged between weekday and weekend prices. Each "$" represents $50. Thus a cost symbol of "$$$" means a room (or suite) at that hotel will cost about $150 a night.

HOW THE HOTELS COMPARE

Hotel	Star Rating	Quality Rating	Cost ($=$50)
Bellagio	★★★★★	96	$$$$$–
Caesars Palace	★★★★½	95	$$$$–
Regent Las Vegas	★★★★½	95	$$$$–
Four Seasons at Mandalay Bay	★★★★½	94	$$$$$$–
Venetian	★★★★½	94	$$$$+
Mandalay Bay	★★★★½	92	$$$$+
Paris	★★★★½	91	$$$
Mirage	★★★★	89	$$$+
Alexis Park	★★★★	88	$$$–
Embassy Suites Convention Center	★★★★	88	$$$–
Hyatt at Lake Las Vegas	★★★★	88	$$$–
Aladdin	★★★★	87	$$–
Las Vegas Hilton	★★★★	87	$$–
MGM Grand	★★★★	87	$$$$–
St. Tropez	★★★★	87	$$–
Embassy Suites in Las Vegas	★★★★	86	$$+
Hard Rock Hotel	★★★★	86	$$$$–
Crowne Plaza	★★★★	85	$$$–
Golden Nugget	★★★★	85	$$+

HOW THE HOTELS COMPARE (continued)

Hotel	Star Rating	Quality Rating	Cost ($=$50)
Rio	★★★★	85	$$$$$–
Marriott Suites	★★★★	84	$$$–
Treasure Island	★★★★	84	$$$+
Residence Inn by Marriott	★★★★	83	$$$–
AmeriSuites	★★★½	82	$$+
Harrah's	★★★½	82	$$+
Luxor	★★★½	82	$$$–
New Frontier (Atrium Tower)	★★★½	82	$+
Sunset Station	★★★½	82	$$+
Bally's	★★★½	81	$$$+
Monte Carlo	★★★½	81	$$$+
Flamingo Hilton	★★★½	80	$+
Candlewood Suites	★★★½	79	$+
Stratosphere	★★★½	79	$+
Sam's Town	★★★½	78	$$–
Castaways	★★★½	77	$–
Courtyard by Marriott	★★★½	77	$$$+
Stardust	★★★½	76	$+
Arizona Charlie's East	★★★½	75	$+
Main Street Station	★★★½	75	$+
New Frontier (Garden Rooms)	★★★½	75	$+
New York–New York	★★★	74	$$+
Palace Station	★★★	74	$$–
Las Vegas Club (North Tower)	★★★	73	$+
Riviera	★★★	73	$$$–
Santa Fe Station	★★★	73	$+
Circus Circus (Tower Rooms)	★★★	72	$$+
The Reserve	★★★	72	$$+
Barbary Coast	★★★	71	$$–
Holiday Inn Emerald Springs	★★★	71	$$+
Texas Station	★★★	70	$$–
Sahara	★★★	69	$+
San Remo	★★★	69	$$–
Boulder Station	★★★	67	$+

HOW THE HOTELS COMPARE (continued)

Hotel	Star Rating	Quality Rating	Cost ($=$50)
California	★★★	67	$+
Comfort Inn South	★★★	67	$$−
Four Queens	★★★	67	$+
Orleans	★★★	67	$$−
Silverton	★★★	67	$−
Tropicana	★★★	67	$$$−
Excalibur	★★★	66	$$+
Fairfield Inn	★★★	66	$$−
Arizona Charlie's West (Klondike Tower)	★★★	65	$+
Best Western Mardi Gras Inn	★★★	65	$$−
Holiday Inn Boardwalk	★★★	65	$$−
Imperial Palace	★★★	65	$$−
Sam Boyd's Fremont	★★★	65	$$−
Bourbon Street	★★½	64	$−
Key Largo Casino	★★½	64	$+
La Quinta	★★½	64	$+
Maxim	★★½	64	$+
Fitzgeralds	★★½	63	$
Hawthorne Inn & Suites	★★½	63	$+
Terrible's	★★½	63	$+
El Cortez	★★½	62	$+
Fiesta	★★½	62	$+
Horseshoe (East Wing)	★★½	61	$−
Arizona Charlie's West (Meadows Tower)	★★½	60	$+
Plaza	★★½	60	$+
Circus Circus (Manor Rooms)	★★½	59	$−
Lady Luck	★★½	59	$−
Nevada Palace	★★½	59	$+
Gold Coast	★★½	58	$$+
Las Vegas Club (South Tower)	★★½	58	$+
Best Western McCarran Inn	★★½	57	$+
Casino Royale	★★½	57	$+

HOW THE HOTELS COMPARE (continued)

Hotel	Star Rating	Quality Rating	Cost ($=$50)
Royal Hotel	★★½	56	$+
Horseshoe (West Wing)	★★	53	$–
Days Inn Downtown	★★	53	$$–
Days Inn Town Hall Casino Hotel	★★	53	$$–
Vacation Village	★★	53	$$–
Howard Johnson Airport	★★	52	$+
Motel 6	★★	52	$+
Super 8	★★	52	$+
Howard Johnson	★★	50	$–
Travelodge Las Vegas Inn	★★	50	$+
Westward Ho	★★	50	$$–
Wild Wild West	★★	49	$

The Top 30 Best Deals in Las Vegas

Having listed the nicest rooms in town, let's reorder the list to rank the best combinations of quality and value in a room. Each lodging property is awarded a value rating on a 0–100 scale. The higher the rating, the better the value.

A ★★½ room at $30 may have the same value rating as a ★★★★ room at $85, but that does not mean the rooms will be of comparable quality. Regardless of whether it's a good deal or not, a ★★½ room is still a ★★½ room.

Listed below are the best room buys for the money, regardless of location or star classification, based on averaged rack rates. Note that sometimes a suite can cost less than a hotel room.

THE TOP 30 BEST DEALS IN LAS VEGAS

Hotel	Star Rating	Value Rating	Quality Rating	Cost ($=$50)
1. Castaways	★★★½	99	77	$–
2. St. Tropez	★★★★	78	87	$$–
3. Main Street Station	★★★½	77	75	$+
4. Stardust	★★★½	76	76	$+

THE TOP 30 BEST DEALS (continued)

Hotel	Star Rating	Value Rating	Quality Rating	Cost ($=$50)
5. Las Vegas Hilton	★★★★	75	87	$$−
6. Stratosphere	★★★½	75	79	$+
7. Silverton	☆★★	72	67	$−
8. New Frontier (Atrium Tower)	★★★½	72	82	$+
9. Aladdin	★★★★	72	87	$$−
10. Candlewood Suites	★★★½	71	79	$+
11. Arizona Charlie's East	★★★½	67	75	$+
12. Flamingo Hilton	★★★½	66	80	$+
13. New Frontier (Garden Rooms)	★★★½	66	75	$+
14. Sahara	★★★	66	69	$+
15. Las Vegas Club (North Tower)	★★★	65	73	$+
16. Circus Circus (Manor Rooms)	★★★	63	59	$−
17. Boulder Station	★★★	60	67	$+
18. Santa Fe Station	★★★	59	73	$+
19. Golden Nugget	★★★★	57	85	$$+
20. Bourbon Street	★★½	57	64	$−
21. Fitzgeralds	★★½	55	63	$
22. Horseshoe (East Wing)	★★½	55	61	$−
23. Four Queens	★★★	54	67	$+
24. Lady Luck	★★½	53	59	$−
25. Sam's Town	★★★½	52	78	$$−
26. Embassy Suites in Las Vegas	★★★★	51	86	$$+
27. California	★★★	50	67	$+
28. Palace Station	★★★	49	74	$$−
29. Arizona Charlie's West (Klondike Tower)	★★★	49	65	$+
30. Paris	★★★★½	48	91	$$$

Leisure, Recreation, and Services Rating of Hotel-Casinos

Many Las Vegas visitors use their hotel rooms as a depository for luggage and a place to nap or shower. These folks are far more interested in what the hotel offers in gambling, restaurants, live entertainment, services, and recreation.

Ranked below for breadth and quality of their offerings are hotels with full casinos. Using a weighted model, we calculated a composite Leisure, Recreation, and Services Rating. The rating should help you determine which properties provide the best over-all vacation or leisure experience.

Interpreting the LR&S Ratings

Some hotels score low because they offer little entertainment, recreation, or food service. If the property is somewhat isolated, these deficiencies pose serious problems. If, on the other hand, a hotel is in a prime location, the shortcomings hardly matter.

Because the LR&S is a composite rating, its primary value is in identifying properties that offer the highest quality and greatest variety of restaurants, diversions, and activities. The rating does not indicate what those restaurants, diversions, or activities are.

LR&S RATING FOR HOTELS WITH FULL CASINOS

Rank	Hotel	Leisure, Recreation & Services Rating
1	Mandalay Bay	97
2	Bellagio	94
3	Caesars Palace	93
4	Mirage	93
5	MGM Grand	91
6	Aladdin	90
7	Rio	90
8	Treasure Island	90
9	Venetian	90
10	Paris	88
11	Luxor	87
12	Las Vegas Hilton	86
13	Flamingo Hilton	83

LR&S RATING (continued)

Rank	Hotel	Leisure, Recreation & Services Rating
14	Bally's	82
15	Monte Carlo	81
16	New York–New York	80
17	Harrah's	79
18	Stratosphere	78
19	Tropicana	78
20	Hard Rock Hotel	77
21	Regent Las Vegas	76
22	Golden Nugget	75
23	Excalibur	74
24	Sunset Station	74
25	Circus Circus	73
26	Orleans	73
27	Imperial Palace	72
28	Riviera	72
29	Sahara	71
30	Sam's Town	70
31	Texas Station	69
32	Main Street Station	68
33	Stardust	68
34	Palace Station	67
35	Santa Fe Station	67
36	New Frontier	66
37	Boulder Station	65
38	Fiesta	65
39	Gold Coast	64
40	Castaways	63
41	Lady Luck	62
42	Four Queens	61
43	Reserve	61
44	Suncoast	61
45	San Remo	60
46	Silverton	60
47	Terrible's	60
48	Barbary Coast	59
49	California	59
50	Plaza	58
51	Arizona Charlie's East	57

LR&S RATING (continued)

Rank	Hotel	Leisure, Recreation & Services Rating
52	Arizona Charlie's West	56
53	Horseshoe	56
54	Sam Boyd's Fremont	55
55	Las Vegas Club	54
56	Holiday Inn Boardwalk	53
57	Fitzgeralds	51
58	Nevada Palace	51
59	Westward Ho	51
60	Casino Royale	46
61	Wild Wild West	46
62	Bourbon Street	45
63	Days Inn Town Hall Casino	38
64	Vacation Village	38
65	El Cortez	31

When Only the Best Will Do

The trouble with profiles, including ours, is that details and distinctions are sacrificed in the interest of brevity and information accessibility. To distinguish the exceptional from the average, here are some best-of lists.

Best Dining (Expense No Issue)

1. Bellagio
2. Paris
3. Caesars Palace
4. Mandalay Bay
5. Venetian
6. Mirage
7. Rio
8. Aladdin

Best Dining (For Great Value)

1. Orleans
2. Suncoast
3. Main Street Station
4. Palace Station
5. Regent Las Vegas
6. Excalibur
7. California
8. Fiesta Station
9. Horseshoe
10. Boulder Station

Best Buffets
1. Sam's Town
2. Aladdin
3. Bellagio
4. Paris Le Village
5. Rio
6. Reserve
7. Orleans
8. Main Street
9. Fiesta
10. Sunset Station

Best Champagne Brunches
1. Bally's
2. MGM Grand (Brown Derby)
3. Circus Circus
4. Fiesta
5. MGM Grand (House of Blues)
6. Caesars Palace

Most Romantic Hotel-Casinos
1. Rio
2. Caesars Palace
3. Mirage
4. Mandalay Bay
5. Venetian

Best Guest-Room Baths
1. Caesars Palace
2. Bellagio
3. Venetian
4. Rio
5. Orleans

Most Visually Interesting Casinos
1. Luxor
2. Venetian
3. Caesars Palace
4. Main Street Station
5. Mandalay Bay
6. Mirage
7. New York–New York
8. Aladdin
9. Sunset Station
10. Rio

Best Views from Guest Rooms
1. Rio
2. Caesars Palace (Palace Tower)
3. Venetian (north-view rooms)
4. Bellagio
5. Mandalay Bay/Four Seasons
6. Stratosphere (upper south-view rooms)
7. Aladdin
8. Tropicana (towers)
9. Hard Rock Hotel
10. New York–New York
11. Fitzgeralds

Best for Shopping On-Site or within a 4-Minute Walk
1. Caesars Palace
2. Venetian
3. Mirage
4. Treasure Island
5. Aladdin

Best for Golf
Regent Las Vegas

Best for Tennis
1. MGM Grand
2 Bally's

Best for Tennis (cont.)
3   Caesars Palace
4. Regent Las Vegas
5. Las Vegas Hilton

Best for Bowling
1. Castaways
2. Gold Coast
3. Sam's Town
4. Orleans
5. Santa Fe Station

Best for Jogging or Running
1. Mandalay Bay
2. Las Vegas Hilton

Best for Ice Skating
Santa Fe Station

Best Spas
1. Venetian
2. Regent Las Vegas
3. Caesars Palace
4. Bellagio
5. Mandalay Bay
6. Mirage
7. Paris
8. Monte Carlo
9. Treasure Island
10. Luxor

Best Swimming & Sunbathing
1. Mandalay Bay
2. Bellagio
3. Caesars Palace
4. Mirage
5. Venetian
6. Treasure Island
7. Tropicana
8. Flamingo
9. Monte Carlo
10. Hard Rock Hotel
11. Rio
12. Las Vegas Hilton
13. MGM Grand
14. Luxor

Best for Weight Lifting, Nautilus, Stationary Cycling, Stair Machines, & Other Indoor Exercise Equipment
1. Venetian
2. Caesars Palace
3. Mandalay Bay
4. Bellagio
5. Mirage
6. Paris
7. Treasure Island
8. MGM Grand
9. Luxor
10. Regent Las Vegas
11. Monte Carlo

Putting the Ratings Together

To complete the picture for hotels with casinos, we combine the Room Quality Rating; the Room Value Rating; and the Leisure, Recreation, and Services Rating to derive an Overall Rating. Guest room considerations (quality and value) account for half of the Overall Rating, while the LR&S Rating accounts for the remaining half.

| | OVERALL RATINGS | | | |
| | 50% LR&S Rating | 25% Quality Rating | 25% Value Rating | 100% Overall Rating |
Hotel				
Aladdin	90	87	72	85
Las Vegas Hilton	86	87	75	84
Caesars Palace	93	95	42	81
Mandalay Bay	97	92	33	80
MGM Grand	91	87	48	79
Mirage	93	89	40	79
Paris	88	91	48	79
Venetian	90	94	40	79
Bellagio	94	96	30	78
Flamingo Hilton	83	80	66	78
Stratosphere	78	79	75	78
Castaways	63	77	99	76
Treasure Island	90	84	35	75
Golden Nugget	75	85	57	73
Luxor	87	82	34	73
Main Street Station	68	75	77	72
Rio	90	85	24	72
Stardust	68	76	76	72
Harrah's	79	82	44	71
Regent Las Vegas	76	95	38	71
New Frontier	66	79	70	70
Bally's	82	81	31	69
Sahara	71	69	67	69
Hard Rock Hotel	77	86	31	68
Monte Carlo	81	81	30	68
New York–New York	80	74	33	67
Sam's Town	70	78	51	67
Santa Fe Station	67	73	60	67
Circus Circus	73	66	50	66

| Hotel | OVERALL RATINGS | | | |
	50% LR&S Rating	25% Quality Rating	25% Value Rating	100% Overall Rating
Silverton	60	67	73	65
Arizona Charlie's East	57	75	67	64
Boulder Station	65	67	60	64
Palace Station	67	74	50	64
Orleans	73	67	37	63
Suncoast	61	82	47	63
Tropicana	78	67	28	63
Imperial Palace	72	65	41	62
Texas Station	69	70	41	62
Excalibur	74	66	28	61
Four Queens	61	67	55	61
Riviera	72	73	28	61
California	59	67	51	59
Fiesta	65	62	42	59
Lady Luck	62	59	53	59
Barbary Coast	59	71	42	58
Las Vegas Club	54	66	55	57
Reserve	61	72	35	57
San Remo	60	69	37	57
Sunset Station	74	52	28	57
Terrible's	60	63	40	56
Arizona Charlie's West	56	63	44	55
Fitzgeralds	51	63	56	55
Horseshoe	56	57	52	55
Plaza	58	60	44	55
Bourbon Street	45	64	58	53
Holiday Inn Boardwalk	53	65	41	53
Sam Boyd's Fremont	55	65	39	53
Gold Coast	64	58	22	52
Nevada Palace	51	59	40	50
Casino Royale	46	57	37	46
Wild Wild West	46	49	35	44
El Cortez	31	62	47	43
Westward Ho	51	50	21	43
Days Inn Town Hall Casino	38	53	24	38
Vacation Village	38	53	20	37

Part Two

Entertainment and Nightlife

Las Vegas Shows and Entertainment

Las Vegas calls itself the "Entertainment Capital of the World." This is arguably true, particularly in terms of the sheer number of live entertainment productions staged daily. Plus, the standard of professionalism and value for your entertainment dollar is very high.

That having been said, here's the bad news: The average price of a ticket to one of the major production shows topped $53 in 2001, a whopping 96% increase since 1992. To balance the picture, however, the standard of quality for shows has likewise soared. And variety, well, there's now literally something for everyone, from traditional Las Vegas feathers and butts to real Broadway musicals. And believe it or not, the value is still there. Maybe not in the grand showrooms and incessantly hyped productions, but in the smaller showrooms and lounges and in the main theaters of off-Strip hotels. Most Las Vegas live entertainment offerings can be categorized as:

Celebrity Headliners	Impersonator Shows
Long-Term Engagements	Comedy Clubs
Production Shows	Lounge Entertainment

Celebrity Headliners   These concerts or shows feature big-name entertainers in a limited engagement, usually one to four weeks, but sometimes a single night. Big-name performers' shows cost $25–90.

Long-Term Engagements   These are shows by the famous and once-famous who have come to Las Vegas to stay.

Production Shows   These are continuously running, Broadway-style theatrical and musical productions. They feature chorus lines, elaborate choreography, and great spectacle. Usually playing twice nightly, six or seven days a week, production shows often run for years. Usually, the show opens with an elaborate number featuring dancers or ice skaters and, often, topless showgirls. Magic or musical numbers then alternate with variety acts, including comics, jugglers, and balancing artists. The show ends with a spectacular finale.

Impersonator Shows   These are usually long-running shows featuring the impersonation of celebrities living (Joan Rivers, Cher, Neil Diamond, Tina Turner, Madonna) and dead (Marilyn Monroe, Elvis, Liberace). Generally, men impersonate male stars and women impersonate female stars.

Comedy Clubs   Stand-up comedy has a long tradition in Las Vegas. With the success of comedy clubs nationwide and the comedy club format on television, stand-up comedy in Las Vegas was elevated from lounges and production shows to its own venues. Las Vegas comedy clubs are small- to medium-sized showrooms featuring two to five comedians per show. Shows usually change each week, and they draw equally among tourists and locals. Most comics are young, and the humor is often raw and scatalogical.

Lounge Entertainment   Many casinos offer exceptional entertainment day and night in their lounges. Musical groups predominate. Reservations aren't required; if you like what you hear, walk in. (Sometimes there's a two-drink minimum for sitting in on a show.) Consult local visitor guides for your preferred music.

They Come and They Go

Las Vegas shows come and go. Don't be surprised if some of the shows reviewed in this guide are gone before you arrive.

Learn Who Is Playing before Leaving Home

The Las Vegas Convention and Visitors Authority publishes *Showguide,* an entertainment calendar for all showrooms and many lounges. The *Showguide* can be obtained without charge by writing or calling:

Las Vegas Convention and Visitors Authority
Visitor Information Center
3150 Paradise Road
Las Vegas, NV 89109-9096
(702) 892-7576 or (702) 892-0711

On the Internet, log onto **ilovevegas.com** and then click on "Limited Engagement."

Show Prices and Taxes

Admission to shows is around $15–100 or more per person. At dinner shows, dinner is extra. Prices usually don't include taxes (17%) or server gratuities.

As recently as 1990, reserved seats were nonexistent. You made your reservation, then arrived early to be assigned a seat by the showroom maître d'. (Slipping the maître d' a tip ensured a better seat.) Typically, the show price included two drinks, and you paid at your table. The current trend is toward reserved seating. Seats are assigned when you buy your tickets at the casino box office or by phone with your credit card. At the showroom, an usher takes you to your seats. If there are two performances per night, the early show is often more expensive. Some shows add a "surcharge" on Saturdays and holidays. Ask about deals and discounts when you call for show or lodging reservations.

How to Make Reservations for Las Vegas Shows

Almost all showrooms take phone reservations. Either you call the reservation numbers we list, or your hotel concierge calls. Most shows accept reservations at least one day in advance.

Some shows take only your name and the number of people in your party. You pay at the box office on the day of the show or in the showroom after you're seated.

Increasingly, shows allow you to prepurchase tickets by phone using a credit card, and you then pick up your tickets at the box office before the show.

Hotel Lobby Ticket Sales

The phone reservation system works perfectly, but some folks prefer to buy tickets at booths operated by independent brokers in hotel lobbies. These visitors pay substantial booking and gratuity surcharges and discover at the showroom that the ticket doesn't guarantee reserved seating. Further, at several showrooms, these tickets must be exchanged for one of the showroom's tickets—after another wait in line. Booths selling seats only for shows at that hotel-casino won't add surcharges.

Trying to See a Show without a Reservation or Ticket
Sunday through Thursday, you have a fair shot at getting into most shows by asking the maitre d' to seat you or by purchasing a ticket at the box office. On most Fridays and Saturdays, however, don't wait in line at the showroom entrance to inquire. Go directly to the box office, maître d', or other show personnel and ask if there's room for your party. You may be asked to join the end of the line or to wait while they check for no-shows or cancellations. An amazing percentage of the time, you'll be admitted.

Dinner Shows
Some dinner shows represent good deals, others less so. Be aware, however, that with all dinner shows, your drinks (if you have any) will be extra, and invariably expensive. Food quality at dinner shows varies. In general it can be characterized as acceptable, but certainly not exceptional. What you are buying is limited-menu banquet service for 300–500 people. Whenever a hotel kitchen tries to feed that many people at once, it is at some cost in terms of the quality of the meal and the service.

Early vs. Late Shows
If you attend a late show, you have time for a leisurely dinner before the performance. If you prefer to eat late, the early show followed by dinner works better. Both shows are identical except that for some productions the early show is covered and the late is topless.

Practical Matters
What to Wear to the Show
For a performance in the main showrooms at Bally's, Bellagio, Caesars Palace, the Flamingo Hilton, Mandalay Bay, or the Mirage, gentlemen will feel more comfortable in sport coats, with

or without neckties. At the Las Vegas Hilton, Venetian, and Bally's, where there is a lot of convention traffic, men would not be overdressed in suits. Women generally wear suits, dresses, skirt and blouse/sweater combinations, and even semiformal attire.

Showrooms at the Luxor, the Stratosphere, Monte Carlo, New York–New York, Treasure Island, the MGM Grand, Harrah's, the Rio, Paris Las Vegas, Tropicana, Aladdin, the Riviera, the Sahara, and the Stardust are a bit less dressy (sport coats are fine, but slacks and sweaters or sport shirts are equally acceptable for men), while showrooms at the Excalibur, the Imperial Palace, the Orleans, Sam's Town, Suncoast, Sunset Station, Texas Station, the House of Blues at Mandalay Bay, the Golden Nugget, and the Hard Rock are the least formal of all (come as you are). All of the comedy clubs are informal, though you would not feel out of place in a sport coat or, for women, a dress.

Invited Guests and Line Passes

At the showroom, guests line up to be seated. At showrooms with reserved seats, patrons are ushered to their seats. At those without, guests normally encounter two lines. The shorter is where "Invited Guests" (gamblers staying at that casino) queue up for immediate seating. Some have been given "comps" (complimentary admission) to the show. If you're giving the casino a lot of action, request a comp.

Gamblers or hotel guests of more modest means frequently receive line passes. These guests pay the standard price for the show but are admitted through the Invited Guest line. To obtain a line pass, tell the floorman or pit boss that you have been gambling a fair amount in their casino and have show reservations. Ask for a line pass. You'll probably get one, especially Sunday through Thursday.

Invited guests should arrive 30 minutes before show time.

Reservations, Tickets, and Maître d' Seating

Many showrooms practice maître d' seating. This means no seats are reserved, except for certain invited guests. When you call for tickets, you'll be listed on the reservations roster, but you won't receive a seat until you appear before the maître d'. At some showrooms, you pay your waiter for everything (show, taxes, drinks) after you have been seated and served.

At comedy clubs and an increasing number of showrooms, you go first to a booth labeled "Tickets," "Reservations," "Box Office," or "Guest Services." After the attendant verifies your reservation, you pay and receive a ticket to show the maître d'. This replaces paying at your table (unless drinks aren't included). The ticket usually doesn't reserve a specific seat or include gratuities.

Showrooms increasingly are switching from maître d' seating to "box office" or "hard" seating. Seat assignments are printed on tickets. Most showrooms issuing reserved-seat tickets allow you to charge them by phone using your credit card, but the quality of seating is at the mercy of the box office. If you buy tickets in person at the box office, however, you can pick among available seats.

SHOWROOMS WHERE SELF-PARKING IS EASY AND CONVENIENT

Hard Rock	Orleans	San Remo
Desert Inn	Stratosphere	

Where to Sit

The best seats in most showrooms are the roomy booths that provide an unencumbered view of the show. The vast majority of seats, however, are at banquet tables—long, narrow tables where a dozen or more guests are squeezed together.

Banquet-table seating generally is right in front of the stage. Next, on a higher tier, is a row of plush booths. These are often reserved for the casino's best customers (sometimes for big tippers). Behind the booths but on the same level are more banquet tables. The pattern continues to the rear wall.

For big production shows on a wide stage (*Siegfried & Roy, Cirque du Soleil,* etc.) or for musical concerts, sit in the middle and back a little. For smaller shows on medium-sized stages (*Lance Burton, Legends in Concert,* etc.), up front is great. This is also true for headliners like Bill Cosby. For female impersonators, the illusion is better if you're back a bit.

At comedy clubs and smaller shows, there are no bad seats, though you'll want to avoid the columns at the Tropicana's *Comedy Stop. Note:* Comedians often incorporate guests sitting down front into the act.

Getting a Good Seat at Showrooms
with Maître d' Seating

1. Arrive Early This is particularly important Friday and Saturday.

2. Go on an Off Night (Sunday through Thursday) During citywide conventions, weekdays may also be crowded.

3. Know Where You Would Like to Sit State your preferences.

4. Understand Your Tipping Options You have three:

- Don't tip.

- Tip the maître d'.

- Tip the captain instead of the maître d'.

Don't tip Politely request a good seat instead of tipping. This option works better in all but a few showrooms, particularly Sunday through Thursday.

On slower nights, the maître d' often distributes patrons equally throughout the showroom to make the audience look larger. On these nights, you may get preferred seats simply by asking.

Tip the maître d' The maître d' is the man or woman in charge of the showroom. Maître d's in better showrooms are powerful and wealthy; some take in as much as $1,650 a night.

If you arrive early and tip $15–20 (per couple) in major showrooms or $5–10 in smaller rooms, you should get decent seats. Tip more on weekends or at popular or sold-out shows. If you arrive late on a busy night, ask if good seats remain before you tip.

Have your tip folded in your hand when you reach the maître d'. Arrange it so he can see how much it is. State your seating preference as you inconspicuously place the bills in his palm.

A variation is to tip with an appropriate denomination of the casino's chips. They cost the same as currency and imply you have been gambling with that denomination. This gesture makes you an insider and a more valued customer.

Tip the captain Tell the maître d' where you would like to sit, but don't offer a tip. Follow the captain to your seats. If they're good, you haven't spent an extra nickel. If you'd like something better, tip the captain and ask to be moved or to have unoccupied seats you see that you prefer.

Before the Show Begins

For years, admission to cocktail shows included two drinks. Recently, this policy has been in flux. Variations are: a cash bar and no table service (to get a drink before the show, walk to the bar and buy it) or drinks included but no table service (exchange your receipt at the bar for drinks).

Most other showrooms offer table service. You obtain drinks from a server. If they're included, the captain will put a receipt or other documentation at your place when you're seated. The server takes it when you order drinks. If drinks aren't included, a menu lists prices. If you're the last seated at a table, don't worry. Your server *will* notice. Depend on your server to advise you when it's time to settle your tab. Until then, don't offer a tip. Most showrooms accept cash, major credit cards, and traveler's checks.

If you have prepaid for admission and drinks, your gratuity may be included. If not, tip the server a dollar or two per person when your drinks arrive. If you aren't sure what's included, ask.

Bladder Matters Most showrooms don't have a rest room. The nearest one may be across the casino. Allow at least 10 minutes for the round-trip.

Selecting a Show

Selecting a Las Vegas show is a matter of timing, budget, taste, and schedule. To find out which shows and headliners are playing before you leave home, call the Las Vegas Convention and Visitors Authority at (702) 892-7576 and ask them to mail you a Las Vegas *Showguide*.

As the post–World War II baby boomers have moved into middle age and comparative affluence, they have become a primary market for Las Vegas. Stars from the "golden days" of rock and roll, as well as folk singers from the 1960s, are turning up in the main showrooms of the Hard Rock and Bally's with great regularity.

Several production shows, however, have broken the mold, in the process achieving a more youthful presentation while maintaining the loyalty of older patrons. *Splash* (Riviera) is a youthful, high-energy show. *Cirque du Soleil's Mystere* (Treasure Island) is an uproarious yet poignant odyssey in the European tradition. Ditto for *Cirque's "O"* at the Bellagio. *Lance Burton* (Monte Carlo) is extremely creative and works well for all ages. *Lord of the Dance* (New York–New York) is also high energy. The two most hip, avant-garde shows in town are *Blue Man Group* (Luxor) and *De la Guarda* (Rio). Both target younger audiences, offering shows that are wild, loud, and conceptually quite different from anything else in town.

Las Vegas Shows for the Under-21 Crowd

Shows spotlighting magic, circus acts, impersonation, and period entertainment are appropriate for younger viewers. Many celebrity headliner shows are fine for children, and a few production shows offer a covered early show for families. Some topless production shows bar anyone younger than 21. Comedy venues usually admit teenagers accompanied by an adult.

The Best Shows in Town: Celebrity Headliners

The talent, presence, drive, and showmanship of many Las Vegas headliners often exceed all expectations, and even performers you think you wouldn't like will delight and amaze you. Also, don't hesitate to take a chance on a headliner unfamiliar to you.

Here are the major celebrity showrooms and their regular headliners.

Hard Rock Hotel—The Joint

Reservations and Information (702) 693-5066 or (702) 226-4650
Frequent Headliners Top current and oldies rock, pop, blues, folk, and world music stars
Usual Show Times 8 p.m.
Approximate Admission Price $15–180
Drinks Included None
Showroom Size 1,800 persons

Description and Comments The stage is high and the floor is on an incline, so visibility is good. Acoustics are excellent, especially in the middle of the floor and in front of the balcony.

Consumer Tips The Hard Rock Hotel box office sells reserved seats to shows at The Joint. You can purchase tickets via phone using your credit card or in person at the box office. Buy your tickets as far in advance as possible.

Las Vegas Hilton—Hilton Theater

Reservations and Information (702) 732-5111 or (800) 222-5361
Frequent Headliners Trisha Yearwood, Johnny Mathis, Engelbert Humperdink, Dwight Yoakam, Wynonna, Tim Conway
Usual Show Times Varies   **Dark** Varies
Approximate Admission Price Varies
Drinks Included None
Showroom Size 1,650 seats

Description and Comments Offerings run the gamut, including rock and country stars as well as top pop singers and comedians.

Consumer Tips The showroom is almost as likely to sell out on a week-day as on a weekend. Reserved seat tickets can be purchased up to four weeks in advance over the phone with a credit card or at the box office.

Mandalay Bay—House of Blues

Reservations and Information (702) 632-7600 or (877) 632-7400; www.hob.com
Frequent Headliners Current and former pop, rock, R&B, reggae, folk, and country stars
Usual Show Times 8 p.m.
Approximate Admission Price $12–100
Drinks Included None
Showroom Size 1,800 seats

Description and Comments House of Blues is a newer Las Vegas concert hall, very different from The Joint at the Hard Rock, with which it competes head-on for performers and concert-goers.

Consumer Tips House of Blues ticket agents are very difficult to get by telephone; to save yourself an exorbitant phone bill, use the toll-free number listed above (and press 4).

Mandalay Bay—Mandalay Bay Theater

Reservations and Information (702) 632-7580
Frequent Headliners Broadway musicals
Usual Show Times 7:30 p.m.   **Dark** Varies

Approximate Admission Price $35–80
Drinks Included None
Showroom Size 1,700 seats

Description and Comments   The theater has hosted a number of traveling Broadway productions. Occasionally the theater is used as a dance or concert venue.

Consumer Tips   With 1,700 seats, it's one-third larger than almost all Broadway houses. The floor and lower mezzanine seats are all good, but the upper mezzanine is pretty far away, especially for the price. If you go, spring for the extra $10 or $20 for the better seats. Tickets can be ordered as far in advance as you want through the Mandalay Bay box office or Ticketmaster (phone (702) 474-4000).

MGM Grand—Garden Arena

Reservations and Information (702) 891-7777 or (800) 646-7787;
www.mgmgrand.com
Frequent Headliners National acts, superstars, televised boxing,
wrestling, and other sporting events
Usual Show Times Varies   **Dark** Varies
Approximate Admission Price Varies
Drinks Included None
Showroom Size 17,157 seats

Description and Comments   This 275,000-square-foot special events center is designed to accommodate everything from sporting events and concerts to major trade exhibitions.

Consumer Tips   Reserved-seat tickets can be purchased one to two months in advance with your credit card by calling the MGM Grand main reservations number or Ticketmaster outlets, for most but not all shows, (phone (702) 474-4000).

MGM Grand—Hollywood Theater

Reservations and Information (800) 646-7787
Frequent Headliners Righteous Brothers, Liza Minnelli, Sheena Easton,
Tom Jones, Don Rickles, Rodney Dangerfield, Engelbert Humperdink
Usual Show Times Varies   **Dark** Varies
Approximate Admission Price $30–95
Drinks Included None
Showroom Size 650 seats

Description and Comments   The Hollywood Theater hosts a wide range of musical and celebrity headliner productions for one- to three-week engagements.

Consumer Tips   Reserved-seat show tickets can be purchased one to two months in advance with your credit card by calling the MGM Grand's main reservations number.

Mirage—Theatre Mirage

Reservations and Information (702) 792-7777 or (800) 963-9634; www.mirage.com
Frequent Headliners *Siegfried & Roy,* Bill Cosby, Kenny Rogers, Paul Anka
Usual Show Times Varies with performer, 7:30 and 11 p.m. for *Siegfried & Roy*   **Dark** Wednesday and Thursday (for *Siegfried & Roy*)
Approximate Admission Price $55–90; $100.50 for *Siegfried & Roy*
Drinks Included 2 (tax, gratuity, and keepsake program included)
Showroom Size 1,500 persons

Description and Comments   The *Siegfried & Roy* illusion and production show is featured at the Theatre Mirage the vast majority of the year.

Consumer Tips   You must purchase tickets one to three days in advance of the performance at the Mirage box office. The only exception is for hotel guests at the Mirage, who are permitted to charge show tickets to their room.

Orleans—Orleans Showroom

Reservations and Information (702) 365-7075
Frequent Headliners Crystal Gayle, Rich Little, The Smothers Brothers
Usual Show Times Varies with performer   **Dark** Varies
Approximate Admission Price Varies with performer
Drinks Included None
Showroom Size 800 seats

Description and Comments   This small but comfortable showroom offers tiered theater seats arranged in a crescent around the stage.

Consumer Tips   This showroom features some great talent at bargain prices. All seats are reserved.

Stardust—Wayne Newton Theater

Reservations and Information (702) 732-6325
Frequent Headliners Wayne Newton, The Pointers, Manhattan Transfer, Marilyn McCoo, and Billy Davis

Usual Show Times Sunday–Thursday, 9 p.m.; Saturday, 8 and 11 p.m.
Dark Friday
Approximate Admission Price $50 (includes tax, tip, and 1 drink)
Drinks Included 1
Showroom Size 620 seats

Description and Comments Vegas veteran Wayne Newton signed a multiyear contract in 2000, bringing headliner entertainment back to the Stardust for the first time in several decades.

Consumer Tips The Wayne Newton Theater is comfortable with good views from all seats.

Production Shows

Las Vegas Premier Production Shows: Comparing Apples and Oranges

Las Vegas production shows are difficult to compare, and audience tastes differ. That said, our rankings reflect our favorites among continuously running shows. This apples-and-oranges comparison is based on each show's impact, vitality, originality, pace, continuity, crescendo, and ability to entertain. Some shows are better than others, but there aren't any real dogs.

Production Show Hit Parade

We don't rate short-run engagements (comedy clubs, comedy theater, and celebrity headliners) and afternoon-only shows. Those we rate also receive a Value Rating:

A Exceptional value, a real bargain

B Good value

C Absolutely fair, you get
exactly what you pay for

D Somewhat overpriced

F Significantly overpriced

Show prices increased again during 2001, resulting in fewer bargains than in previous years.

Here are profiles of all continuously running production shows, alphabetically by show name. Comedy clubs and celebrity headliner showrooms are profiled in separate sections. Prices fluctuate.

PRODUCTION SHOW HIT PARADE

RANK	SHOW	LOCATION	VALUE RATING
1.	Cirque du Soleil's Mystere	Treasure Island	B
2.	Cirque du Soleil's "O"	Bellagio	F
3.	De la Guarda	Rio	B
4.	EFX	MGM Grand	C
5.	Blue Man Group	Luxor	C
6.	Siegfried & Roy	Mirage	D
7.	The Rat Pack Is Back	Sahara	B
8.	Danny Gans	Mirage	D
9.	Legends In Concert	Imperial Palace	A
10.	Lance Burton	Monte Carlo	C
11.	Jubilee!	Bally's	C
12.	Takin' It Uptown w/ Clint Holmes	Harrah's	C
13.	Folies Bergere	Tropicana	C
14.	Andre-Phillippe Gagnon	Venetian	D
15.	Splash	Riviera	B
16.	American Superstars	Stratosphere	A
17.	Tournament of Kings	Excalibur	A
18.	Storm	Mandalay Bay	C
19.	Second City	Flamingo	B
20.	Melinda-First Lady of Magic	Venetian	D
21.	Steve Wyrick	Sahara	B
22.	The Scintas	Rio	C
23.	Bill Acosta: Lasting Impressions	Flamingo	F
24.	Crazy Girls	Riviera	D
25.	La Cage	Riviera	B
26.	Boy-lesque	New Frontier	B
27.	Skintight	Harrah's	D
28.	Men Are From Mars, Women Are From Venus	Flamingo	D
29.	Midnight Fantasy	Luxor	D
30.	Naked Angels	Plaza	D

American Superstars

Type of Show Celebrity impersonator production show
Host Casino and Showroom Stratosphere—Broadway Showroom
Reservations and Information (702) 382-4446 (reservations necessary)
Admission with Taxes $25.25 (ages 5–12); $32.95 (adults)
Cast Size Approximately 24
Nights of Lowest Attendance Sunday and Monday
Usual Show Times 7 and 10 p.m. Wednesday, Friday, and Saturday; 7 p.m.
Sunday, Monday, and Tuesday   **Dark** Thursday
Special Comments Much enhanced on the larger stage
Topless No
Author's Rating ★★★ ½
Overall Appeal by Age Group

Under 21	21–37	38–50	51 and older
★★★	★★★½	★★★★	★★★½

Duration of Presentation An hour and a half

Description and Comments   *American Superstars* is a fun, upbeat show.
While the impersonations are, in general, not as crisp or realistic as those of
Legends in Concert, the show exhibits a lot of drive and is a great night's
entertainment.

Consumer Tips   Though tickets must be purchased in advance, seat assign-
ment is at the discretion of the maître d'. Drinks are not included but can be
purchased at a bar outside the showroom. *Note:* A $38 package is available
including the show, drinks, buffet dinner, and tickets to the Tower.

Andre-Phillipe Gagnon

Type of Show Musical impressionist
Host Casino and Showroom Venetian—The Showroom
Reservations and Information (702) 414-4300
Admission with Taxes $75–100
Cast Size 6 (not counting Celine Dion)
Night of Lowest Attendance Sunday
Usual Show Times 8:30 p.m.   Dark: Tuesday and Thursday
Topless No
Author's Rating ★★★
Overall Appeal by Age Group

Under 21	21–37	38–50	51 and older
★★★	★★★ ½	★★★★	★★★★

Duration of Presentation An hour and a half

Description and Comments A recent French-Canadian import, Andre-Phillipe Gagnon runs a close second only to Danny Gans as the best impressionist in Las Vegas. The show closes with Gagnon rendering a duet with the looming videotaped image and voice of fellow Canadian Celine Dion.

Consumer Tips Though this venue has fewer seats and about the same prices as the Danny Gans show at the Mirage, it's probably still an easier ticket to get due to Gans' extreme popularity.

Bill Acosta: Lasting Impressions

Type of Show Musical impressionist with some topless dancers
Host Casino and Showroom Flamingo—Bugsy's Theater
Reservations and Information (702) 733-3333
Admission with Taxes $49.95–69.95
Cast Size 18
Night of Lowest Attendance Tuesday (late show)
Usual Show Times 10 p.m. (also 7:30 p.m. on Tuesday)   **Dark** Friday
Topless Yes
Author's Rating ★★½
Overall Appeal by Age Group

Under 21	21–37	38–50	51 and older
—	★★★	★★★½	★★★★

Duration of Presentation An hour and 20 minutes

Description and Comments Bill Acosta is a solid, old-school Las Vegas impressionist. The standout routine is a startling "12 days of impressions," where Acosta rockets between voices as disparate as Ross Perot, Garth Brooks, Jack Nicholson, and more, all within seconds.

Consumer Tips Less expensive than either Danny Gans or Andre-Phillipe Gagnon, Acosta's show hearkens back to the glitzier Vegas shows of yesteryear (there's even a golden staircase).

Blue Man Group

Type of Show Performance art production show
Host Casino and Showroom Luxor—Luxor Theatre
Reservations and Information (702) 262-4400 or (800) 557-7428
Admission with Taxes $79 for floor seats, $69 for balcony seats
Cast Size 3 plus a 15-piece band
Nights of Lowest Attendance Sunday and Monday
Usual Show Times Sunday and Monday 7 p.m., Wednesday–Saturday 7 and 10 p.m.   **Dark** Tuesday
Topless No

Special Comments Teenagers should like this show, but the loud music and dark colors could scare small children

Author's Rating ★★★★

Overall Appeal by Age Group

Under 21	21–37	38–50	51 and older
★★★★	★★★★ ½	★★★★	★★★ ½

Duration of Presentation 1 hour and 45 minutes

Description and Comments The three blue men are just that—blue—and bald and mute. Their fast-paced show uses music and multi-media effects to make light of contemporary art and life in the information age. While the three blue men are the focus of the show, their antics are augmented by a 15-piece band and plenty of audience participation.

Consumer Tips This show is decidedly different and requires an open mind to appreciate. It also helps to be a little loose, because like it or not, everybody gets sucked into the production.

Bottoms Up

Type of Show Bawdy song, dance, and comedy
Host Casino and Showroom Flamingo—Bugsy's Theater
Reservations and Information (702) 733-3333
Admission with Taxes $14 (includes 1 drink)
Cast Size 10
Usual Show Times 2 p.m. and 4 p.m. daily
Special Comments The only afternoon topless show in Las Vegas
Topless Yes
Author's Rating ½
Overall Appeal by Age Group

Under 21	21–37	38–50	51 and older
—	★	★½	★★

Duration of Presentation 1 hour (though it seems much longer)

Description and Comments Imagine an ultra-corny series of excruciatingly stale comedy sketches, periodically interrupted by smarmy stand-up or awful lip-synched show tunes rendered by the wizened core performers.

Consumer Tips If it's imperative that you see a topless show in the afternoon, at least this one is very cheap. Otherwise, avoid *Bottoms Up* at all costs.

Cirque du Soleil's Mystere

Type of Show Circus as theater
Host Casino and Showroom Treasure Island—*Cirque du Soleil* Showroom

Reservations and Information (702) 894-7722 or (800) 392-1999
Admission with Taxes $88
Cast Size 75
Nights of Lowest Attendance Thursday
Usual Show Times 7:30 and 10:30 p.m. **Dark** Monday and Tuesday
Special Comments No table service (no tables!)
Topless No
Author's Rating ★★★★½
Overall Appeal by Age Group

Under 21	21–37	38–50	51 and older
★★★★	★★★★★	★★★★★	★★★★½

Duration of Presentation An hour and a half

Description and Comments *Mystere* is a far cry from a traditional circus but retains all of the fun and excitement. It is whimsical, mystical, and sophisticated, yet pleasing to all ages.

Consumer Tips Be forewarned that the audience is an integral part of *Mystere* and that at almost any time you might be plucked from your seat to participate. Because *Mystere* is presented in its own customized showroom, there are no tables and, consequently, no drink service.

Cirque du Soleil's "O"

Type of Show Circus and aquatic ballet as theater
Host Casino and Showroom Bellagio—Bellagio Theater
Reservations and Information (702) 693-7722
Admission with Taxes $121 main floor; $99 balcony
Cast Size 74
Nights of Lowest Attendance Sunday and Monday
Usual Show Times 7:30 and 10:30 p.m. **Dark** Wednesday and Thursday
Topless No
Author's Rating ★★★★
Overall Appeal by Age Group

Under 21	21–37	38–50	51 and older
★★★★	★★★★★	★★★★★	★★★★ ½

Duration of Presentation An hour and a half

Description and Comments The title *"O"* is a play on words derived from the concept of infinity, with 0 (zero) as its purest expression, and from the phonetic pronunciation of *eau*, the French word for water. The foundation for *"O"* resides in a set that in mere seconds transforms seamlessly into anything from a fountain to a puddle to a vast pool.

Consumer Tips   If you've never seen either of the Las Vegas *Cirque du Soleil* productions, we recommend catching *Mystere* first. For starters, it's $33 per person less expensive and, in our opinion, just as good (if not a smidge better).

Crazy Girls

Type of Show Erotic dance and adult comedy
Host Casino and Showroom Riviera—Mardi Gras Showrooms, second floor
Reservations and Information (702) 794-9301 or (800) 634-3420
Admission with Taxes $25
Cast Size 8
Nights of Lowest Attendance Wednesday
Usual Show Times 8:30 and 10:30 p.m., with a midnight show on Saturdays   **Dark** Monday
Topless Yes
Author's Rating ★★★½
Overall Appeal by Age Group

Under 21	21–37	38–50	51 and older
—	★★★½	★★★½	★★★½

Duration of Presentation 1 hour

Description and Comments   This is a no-nonsense show for men who do not want to sit through jugglers, magicians, and half the score from *Oklahoma!* before they see naked women. The focus is on eight engaging, talented, and athletically built young ladies who bump and grind through an hour of exotic dance and comedy.

Consumer Tips   The show is not really as dirty as the Riviera would lead you to believe, and the nudity does not go beyond topless and G-strings. Men looking for total nudity should try the Palomino Club in North Las Vegas.

Danny Gans: Entertainer of the Year

Type of Show Impressions and variety
Host Casino and Showroom Mirage—Danny Gans Theater
Reservations and Information (702) 791-7111 or (800) 963-9634
Admission with Taxes $75–99
Cast Size Approximately 7
Nights of Lowest Attendance Wednesday
Usual Show Times 8 p.m.   **Dark** Monday and Friday
Topless No
Author's Rating ★★★★

Overall Appeal by Age Group

Under 21	21–37	38–50	51 and older
★★★	★★★½	★★★★	★★★★

Duration of Presentation An hour and 10 minutes

Description and Comments   This "man of many voices" is a monster talent. He does upwards of a hundred impressions during the show. Danny Gans is the best of the solo impressionists working Las Vegas showrooms.

Consumer Tips The show is more of an auditory than a visual experience, so leave the $99 seats (the first eight rows) and be happy with the $75 seats. The Mirage is a bustling place in the evenings so allow an extra 15 minutes to park and get to the showroom.

De la Guarda

Type of Show Interactive Melee'
Host Casino and Showroom Rio—De la Guarda Theatre
Reservations and Information (702) 252-7776
Admission with Taxes $45
Cast Size 14
Nights of Lowest Attendance Wednesday and Thursday
Usual Show Times 9 p.m. Tuesday–Friday; 8 and 10:30 p.m. Saturday
Dark Sunday and Monday
Topless No
Author's Rating ★★★★ ½
Overall Appeal By Age Group

Under 21	21–37	38–50	51 and older
★★★★ ½	★★★★ ½	★★★★ ½	★★★★

Duration of Presentation About an hour

Description and Comments   "The audience must stand through the whole presentation and you may get wet." Both true. When you ask what the show is about you're told that it's really not about anything. In fact, trying to understand De la Guarda at all is a needless waste of energy. The best way to experience De la Guarda is to clear your mind and just let it wash over you.

Consumer Tips   Older patrons love it as much as Gen X'ers. Standing is not a problem; you are so completely engrossed that you'd willingly stand an additional hour. As for getting wet, you can avoid the water by moving around a bit.

EFX!

Type of Show Grand-scale musical production show
Host Casino and Showroom MGM Grand—Grand Theater

Reservations and Information (702) 891-7777 or (800) 929-1111
Admission with Taxes $55 general admission, $75 preferred admission
Cast Size 70
Nights of Lowest Attendance Wednesday and Thursday
Usual Show Times 7:30 and 10:30 p.m.   **Dark** Sunday and Monday
Special Comments Children's admission is $40 ages 5–12
Topless No
Author's Rating ★★★★ ½
Overall Appeal by Age Group

Under 21	21–37	38–50	51 and older
★★★	★★★★ ½	★★★★ ½	★★★★

Duration of Presentation An hour and a half

Description and Comments   In *EFX!* Rick Springfield guides the audience through an animatronic (robotic) and technological odyssey that is reported to have cost $30 million to produce.

Consumer Tips   The better seats for *EFX!* are back about four tiers from the front and in the center. We recommend booking your seats a couple of weeks in advance.

An Evening at La Cage

Type of Show Female-impersonator revue
Host Casino and Showroom Riviera—Mardi Gras Showrooms, third floor
Reservations and Information (702) 794-9433 or (800) 634-3420
Admission with Taxes $25
Cast Size Approximately 20
Nights of Lowest Attendance Sunday and Monday
Usual Show Times 7:30 and 9:30 p.m.   **Dark** Tuesday
Topless No
Author's Rating ★★★
Overall Appeal by Age Group

Under 21	21–37	38–50	51 and older
—	★★★½	★★★	★★★

Duration of Presentation An hour and 15 minutes

Description and Comments   *La Cage* re-creates the female-impersonator revue made famous by productions of the same name in New York and Los Angeles. A high-tempo show with a great sense of humor, *La Cage* is at once outrageous, lusty, weird, and sensitive.

Consumer Tips   *La Cage* and *Boy-lesque* (New Frontier) are similar in both content and quality. If you see one it would be redundant to see the other.

Seating is by the maître d'. Once seated, you fetch your own drinks from the bar using your ticket stub as a voucher.

Folies Bergere (The Best of)

Type of Show Music, dance, and variety production show
Host Casino and Showroom Tropicana—Tiffany Theater
Reservations and Information (702) 739-2411 or (800) 634-4000
Admission with Taxes $51.45 general; $62.45 VIP
Cast Size Approximately 90
Nights of Lowest Attendance Monday, Tuesday, and Sunday
Usual Show Times 7:30 p.m (allows ages 5 and up) and 10 p.m.
Dark Thursday
Topless Late show only
Author's Rating ★★★
Overall Appeal by Age Group

Under 21	21–37	38–50	51 and older
★★	★★★	★★★	★★★★

Duration of Presentation An hour and a half

Description and Comments *Folies Bergere* is pretty much what you would expect: exotically clad (or unclad) showgirls and cancan dancers, chorus lines, singers, and music with a fin-de-sieclé French cabaret feel.

Consumer Tips There is a lot more booth seating than in most showrooms and a good view from practically every seat in the house. No drinks come with the price of the show. If you need to use the distant rest room before the show, allow yourself plenty of time.

Hot Trix

Type of Show Topless revue with comic and magician
Host Casino and Showroom Plaza—Plaza Theater
Reservations and Information (702) 386-2444
Admission with Taxes $30 (includes 1 drink)
Cast Size Approximately 8
Night of Lowest Attendance Thursday
Usual Show Times 8 and 10 p.m. **Dark** Monday
Topless Yes
Author's Rating ★★½
Overall Appeal by Age Group

Under 21	21–37	38–50	51 and older
—	★★ ½	★★★	★★★

Duration of Presentation An hour and 20 minutes

Description and Comments   The full name of this production is "Hot Trix with Special Guest Peter Barbutti and Karen Denise's Naked Angels." Barbutti is a lounge lizard in true Las Vegas style. Barbutti serves as dirty ol' elder statesman to Karen Denise and her Naked Angels, who share the stage with him about half the time.

Consumer Tips   Sightlines in this small venue are slightly obstructed at the extreme front left and right. Discount coupons are available at the casino and in visitor magazines.

Jubilee!

Type of Show   Grand-scale musical and variety production show

Host Casino and Showroom   Bally's—The Jubilee Theater
Reservations and Information   (702) 967-4567 or (800) 237-SHOW
Admission with Taxes $52–62.50 ($2.50 extra on credit card purchase)
Cast Size   100
Nights of Lowest Attendance   Sunday and Thursday
Usual Show Times   7:30 and 10:30 p.m.   **Dark**   Tuesday
Topless   Yes
Author's Rating   ★★★★
Overall Appeal by Age Group

Under 21	21–37	38–50	51 and older
★★★	★★★	★★★½	★★★★

Duration of Presentation   An hour and a half

Description and Comments   Jubilee! is the quintessential, traditional Las Vegas production show. With a cast of 100, two multiscene production extravaganzas top the list of Jubilee! highlights. The first is the sultry saga of Samson and Delilah, climaxing with Samson's destruction of the temple. The second is the story of the Titanic, from launch to sinking.

Consumer Tips   Banquet tables at the foot of the stage are too close and cramped; a row of booths above the tables are more expensive but worth it. Otherwise take one of the 789 theater-style seats.

Lance Burton: Master Magician

Type of Show   Magical illusion with dancing and specialty acts
Host Casino and Showroom   Monte Carlo—Lance Burton Theatre
Reservations and Information   (702) 730-7000 or (800) 311-8999
Admission with Taxes $54.95 balcony; $59.95 main floor
Cast Size   14
Nights of Lowest Attendance   Thursday and Friday

Usual Show Times 7 and 10 p.m.   **Dark** Sunday and Monday
Special Comments No drinks included
Topless No
Author's Rating ★★★★
Overall Appeal by Age Group

Under 21	21–37	38–50	51 and older
★★★★	★★★★	★★★★	★★★★

Duration of Presentation An hour and a half

Description and Comments   Lance Burton displays some extraordinary sleight of hand in a repertoire of illusions that cannot be seen in other showrooms. Augmented by comely assistants, a comedic juggler, and a talented dance troupe, Lance Burton delivers quality entertainment.

Consumer Tips   The venue is so large that it's hard to appreciate Burton's exquisite and subtle sleight of hand if you are seated in the boonies. Try to get seats on the main floor close to the stage.

Legends in Concert

Type of Show Celebrity-impersonator and musical production show
Host Casino and Showroom Imperial Palace—Imperial Theatre
Reservations and Information (702) 794-3261
Admission with Taxes $34.50 adults (includes tax, 2 drinks, and tip);
$19.50 children (ages 12 and under)
Cast Size Approximately 20
Nights of Lowest Attendance Wednesday and Thursday
Usual Show Times 7:30 and 10:30 p.m.   **Dark** Sunday
Topless No
Author's Rating ★★★★
Overall Appeal by Age Group

Under 21	21–37	38–50	51 and older
★★★★	★★★★	★★★★	★★★★

Duration of Presentation An hour and a half

Description and Comments   The show is a barn-burner and possibly, minute-for-minute, the fastest-moving show in town. The impersonations are extremely effective, replicating the physical appearances, costumes, mannerisms, and voices of the celebrities with remarkable likeness.

Consumer Tips   Admission includes two drinks. Payment must be made at the box office any time prior to the show. Arrive 40 minutes before show time for seating by the maître d'. Make your reservations early.

Melinda

Type of Show Magic and Illusion

Host Casino and Showroom Venetian—Showroom at the Venetian

Reservations and Information (702) 948-3007

Admission with Taxes $38–77

Cast Size 12

Nights of Lowest Attendance Sunday and Monday

Usual Show Times 6:30 and 8:30 p.m. Monday and Friday–Sunday; 6:30 p.m. Tuesday and Thursday

Topless No

Author's Rating ★★★

Overall Appeal by Age Group

Under 21	21–37	38–50	51 and older
★★★★	★★★ ½	★★★ ½	★★★ ½

Duration of Presentation An hour and ten minutes

Description and Comments   Although Melinda doesn't break any new ground, her illusions are solid, and some of her props (a giant industrial drill on which she is impaled comes to mind) almost deserve a show of their own.

Consumer Tips   Melinda puts on a good show, but it's overpriced. You'll get better illusion and do less damage to your wallet at the Sahara (Steve Wyrick) or the Monte Carlo (Lance Burton).

Men Are from Mars, Women Are from Venus

Type of Show Broadway-style musical comedy

Host Casino and Showroom Flamingo

Reservations and Information (702) 733-3333

Admission with Taxes $36, $44, $52

Cast Size 10 plus musicians

Nights of Lowest Attendance Sunday and Thursday

Usual Show Times 7:30 p.m. Monday, Wednesday, Thursday, and Saturday; 7:30 and 10 p.m. Friday; 3 and 7:30 p.m. Sunday

Topless No

Author's Rating ★★

Overall Appeal by Age Group

Under 21	21–37	38–50	51 and older
★★	★★ ½	★★ ½	★★ ½

Duration of Presentation About an hour and a half (seems longer)

Description and Comments *Men Are from Mars, Women Are from Venus* is a musical comedy about male/female relationships. We recommend you forget the show and read the book of the same name.

Consumer Tips If for some reason you decide to see this show, purchase the least expensive ticket.

Michael Flatley's Lord of the Dance

Type of Show Celtic music and dance production
Host Casino and Showroom New York–New York—Broadway Theater
Reservations and Information (702) 740-6815
Admission with Taxes $59 Tuesday–Thursday; $68 Friday and Saturday
Cast Size 44
Nights of Lowest Attendance Wednesday
Usual Show Times 7 and 10 p.m. Tuesday and Wednesday; 9 p.m. Thursday and Friday; 3 and 8 p.m. Saturday   **Dark** Sunday and Monday
Special Comments Michael Flatley does not dance
Topless No
Author's Rating Rollicking fun; ★★★★
Overall Appeal by Age Group

Under 21	21–37	38–50	51 and older
★★★★	★★★★	★★★★	★★★★

Duration of Presentation An hour and a half

Description and Comments With its jubilant score, relentless pace, and exacting precision, *Lord of the Dance* is decidedly an upper—an evening's entertainment that leaves you curiously both energized and drained. We like *Lord of the Dance* and think you will too.

Consumer Tips If you've seen a live performance of *Riverdance, Lord of the Dance* is essentially more of the same. If you've seen *Riverdance* only on video and liked it, we heartily recommend *Lord of the Dance*. The live production (of either show) has an impact and presence that can only be imagined by watching a video.

Midnight Fantasy

Type of Show Topless dance and comedy revue
Host Casino and Showroom Luxor—Luxor Live Theater
Reservations and Information (702) 262-4400
Admission with Taxes $29.95
Cast Size Approximately 8
Nights of Lowest Attendance Wednesday and Thursday
Usual Show Times 8:30 p.m. Tuesday, Thursday, Saturday, and Sunday; 10:30 p.m. Tuesday–Saturday   **Dark** Monday

Topless Yes
Author's Rating ★★★
Overall Appeal by Age Group

Under 21	21–37	38–50	51 and older
—	★★★	★★½	★★

Duration of Presentation An hour and 15 minutes

Description and Comments   There's some half-naked cavorting, of course, but not as much as one might think from the suggestive nature of the show. And despite the panting over the loudspeakers, the dancing is not particularly erotic.

Consumer Tips   Tickets for Midnight Fantasy must be purchased or picked up at the box office on the second floor of the Luxor, not at the one off the main casino floor.

The Rat Pack Is Back

Type of Show Celebrity impersonator
Host Casino and Showroom Sahara—Congo Room
Reservations and Information (702) 737-2515
Admission with Taxes $41
Cast Size 20 including musicians
Nights of Lowest Attendance Wednesday and Thursday
Usual Show Times 7:30 and 10 p.m. Tuesday and Saturday; 8 p.m. Wednesday, Thursday, Friday, and Sunday
Topless No
Author's Rating ★★★★
Overall Appeal By Age Group

Under 21	21–37	38–50	51 and older
★★ ½	★★★ ½	★★★★	★★★★½

Duration of Presentation An hour and 20 minutes

Description and Comments   The heart and soul of the original Rat Pack were crooners Frank Sinatra, Dean Martin, and Sammy Davis Jr., and comedian Joey Bishop. *The Rat Pack Is Back* recreates a night when the acerbic Bishop and hard-drinking Martin team up with Davis and Sinatra. Backed by a piano, bass, and drums trio, along with a 12-piece horn section, four talented impersonators take you back to a night at the Copa Room in 1963. The impersonations are riveting, almost spooky.

Consumer Tips   *The Rat Pack Is Back* is one of the few true bargains in the Las Vegas galaxy of shows. Seats are assigned by the maître d', but for a $5 tip you can score just about any seat not reserved for the casino's high rollers. Ask for something about midway back.

Scintas

Type of Show Musical and comedy review
Host Casino and Showroom Rio—Copacabana Showroom
Reservations and Information (702) 252-7776 or (800) PLAY-RIO
Admission with Taxes $38.50
Cast Size 4
Nights of Lowest Attendance Monday and Tuesday
Usual Show Times 8 p.m. Monday, Tuesday, Friday, and Sunday; 6 and 8:30 p.m. Saturday   **Dark** Wednesday and Thursday
Topless No
Author's Rating ★★★
Overall Appeal by Age Group

Under 21	21–37	38–50	51 and older
★★	★★★	★★★½	★★★½

Duration of Presentation An hour and a half

Description and Comments   Though the Scintas are also billed as a comedy troupe, they shine most when playing music. With a heavy emphasis on God and patriotism, this show would be more at home in Branson, Missouri.

Consumer Tips   Less than $40, Scintas tickets are reasonably priced even though they don't include drinks or tips.

Second City

Type of Show Sketch Comedy
Host Casino and Showroom Flamingo—Bugsy's Celebrity Theatre
Reservations and Information (702) 733-3333
Admission with Taxes $27.50
Cast Size 5
Nights of Lowest Attendance Monday and Tuesday
Usual Show Times 8 and 10:30 p.m. nightly
Topless No
Author's Rating ★★★★
Overall Appeal by Age Group

Under 21	21–37	38–50	51 and older
★★★½	★★★★	★★★★	★★★★

Duration of Presentation An hour and 15 minutes

Description and Comments   *Second City* is an amazingly talented lot individually and complement and balance each other well as a team. They do a crack job on the improvisational stuff, taking their cues from audience suggestions, but it's their set pieces that really demonstrate their genius.

Consumer Tips   Seating is by the maître d'. Because there really aren't any bad seats, tipping the maître d' is a waste of money unless you want to be right next to the stage.

Siegfried & Roy

Type of Show Magic and illusion show with choreography and spectacle
Host Casino and Showroom Mirage—Siegfried & Roy Theatre
Reservations and Information (702) 792-7777 or (800) 456-4564
Admission with Taxes $100.50 (includes 2 drinks and gratuity)
Cast Size Approximately 88
Nights of Lowest Attendance Sunday and Monday
Usual Show Times 7:30 and 11 p.m. Tuesday, Friday, Saturday; 7:30 p.m.
Sunday and Monday   **Dark** Wednesday and Thursday
Special Comments All gratuities included in admission price
Topless No
Author's Rating ★★★★
Overall Appeal by Age Group

Under 21	21–37	38–50	51 and older
★★★★★	★★★★★	★★★★★	★★★★★

Duration of Presentation An hour and 40 minutes

Description and Comments   The sets and special effects in this show are beyond belief, even overwhelming, with their rich profusion of color, shape, and image. But the presentation is still tasteful and sophisticated. If there is a problem with *Siegfried & Roy,* it is the same problem that plagues most Las Vegas magic-illusion shows: redundancy.

Consumer Tips   Even at $100 a pop in a theater with 1,500 seats, *Siegfried & Roy* sells out almost every night. The best way to see *Siegfried & Roy* on short notice with the least hassle is to set your sights for the late show on a Sunday, Monday, or Tuesday. Since all seats are reserved, you do not have to tip the maître d' or the captains.

Skintight

Type of Show Topless dance show
Host Casino and Showroom Harrah's—Harrah's Showroom
Reservations and Information (702) 369-5111
Admission with Taxes $42
Cast Size Approximately 16
Nights of Lowest Attendance Sunday and Tuesday
Usual Show Times 7:30 p.m. Wednesday; 10:30 p.m. Sunday, Monday,
Tuesday, Friday; and midnight Saturday   **Dark** Thursday

Special Comments This is the only topless show permitting ages 18 and up, as opposed to ages 21 and up

Topless Yes

Author's Rating ★★★½

Overall Appeal by Age Group

Under 21	21–37	38–50	51 and older
★★★★*	★★★ ½	★★★	★★

* Under 18 not permitted

Duration and Presentation An hour and a half

Description and Comments *Skintight* has aspirations to put on a bitchin' dance party. To that end, there's lots of pounding rock-and-pop dance numbers, and skin is frequently visible and widespread among the buff female and male cast.

Consumer Tips Sitting near the center aisle seems to increase one's chances of being selected for onstage antics. Discount coupons are available in the Harrah's casino and in visitor magazines.

Splash

Type of Show Musical variety aquacade show

Host Casino and Showroom Riviera—Versailles Theater

Reservations and Information (702) 794-9301 or (800) 634-3420

Admission with Taxes $58 VIP, $47 general

Cast Size Approximately 50

Nights of Lowest Attendance Sunday, Tuesday, Wednesday

Usual Show Times 7:30 and 10:30 p.m. daily

Special Comments No drinks included

Topless Late show only

Author's Rating ★★★

Overall Appeal by Age Group

Under 21	21–37	38–50	51 and older
★★★	★★★½	★★★½	★★★

Duration of Presentation An hour and a half

Description and Comments The show is held together by a thin thread: a super-submarine visits the North Pole, the Bermuda Triangle, and Atlantis. On the way, though, it pauses at so many ports—four rip-roaring production numbers and a good dozen gimmicks and variety acts—that you wonder if anyone is steering the thing.

Consumer Tips All seats are reserved and assigned in the order in which the reservations are received; the earlier you buy, the better your seats will be. Glassware is not allowed in the showroom. You must carry in your own fluid refreshments in plastic cups.

Steve Wyrick, World-Class Magician

Type of Show Magic and illusion production show
Host Casino and Showroom Sahara—Sahara Theatre
Reservations and Information (702) 737-2515 after 4:30 p.m. PST
Admission with Taxes $41
Cast Size Approximately 12
Nights of Lowest Attendance Sunday and Thursday
Usual Show Times 7:30 and 10:30 p.m.   **Dark** Tuesday
Special Comments Top magic show for the ticket price
Topless No
Author's Rating ★★★½
Overall Appeal by Age Group

Under 21	21–37	38–50	51 and older
★★★½	★★★½	★★★½	★★★½

Duration of Presentation An hour and 15 minutes

Description and Comments   *Steve Wyrick, World-Class Magician* is the Las Vegas show scene's version of "we try harder." Wyrick digs deep and delivers some great illusion and sleight of hand that you won't see in other showrooms.

Consumer Tips   You can't beat Wyrick's show for innovation or value. Compared to *Lance Burton* and *Siegfried & Roy,* Wyrick is a bargain at $41.

Storm

Type of Show Special effects show set to Latin music
Host Casino and Showroom Mandalay Bay–Storm Theatre
Reservations and Information (702) 632-7580 or (877) 632-7400
Admission with Taxes $60.50–71.50
Cast Size 50
Nights of Lowest Attendance Sunday and Thursday
Usual Show Times 7:30 p.m. Sunday, Monday, Wednesday, Thursday, and Saturday; 10:30 p.m. Wednesday, Friday, and Saturday   **Dark** Tuesday
Topless No
Author's Rating ★★½
Overall Appeal by Age Group

Under 21	21–37	38–50	51 and older
★★★★*	★★★½	★★½	★★

*Under 10 years old not admitted

Duration of Presentation An hour and a half

Description and Comments   Storm is ostensibly a show about the interaction of four natural forces—Fire, Ice, Wind, and Earth. There's no doubt that it's a dazzling, tightly run show, with plenty of flash. However, it's also a pretty incoherent mishmash of repeated climaxes and showstopping crescendos.

Consumer Tips   VIP seats can make a dramatic difference in your experience. Props, effects, and other nearby technical gadgets also make lower-auditorium guests feel more included in the production.

Takin' it Uptown Starring Clint Holmes

Type of Show Live concert by Clint Holmes
Host Casino and Showroom Harrah's—Harrah's Main Showroom
Reservations and Information (702) 369-5111 or (800) 392-9002
Admission with Taxes $50
Cast Size 14
Nights of Lowest Attendance Monday and Tuesday
Usual Show Times 7:30 p.m. Monday–Wednesday and Friday; 10 p.m. Thursday and Saturday   **Dark** Sunday
Topless No
Author's Rating ★★★½
Overall Appeal by Age Group

Under 21	21–37	38–50	51 and older
★★½	★★★½	★★★★	★★★½

Duration of Presentation An hour and a half

Description and Comments   Locals and tourists alike will appreciate this show, which epitomizes the trend toward family-friendly entertainment on the strip. You really could bring your children to this show and feel good about it, even if the sophisticated set-list will be most appreciated by those in their 40s and 50s.

Consumer Tips   Harrah's Main Showroom has some booths and some free-standing chairs. The chairs are horribly uncomfortable, so ask for a booth.

Tournament of Kings

Type of Show Jousting and medieval pageant
Host Casino and Showroom Excalibur—King Arthur's Arena
Reservations and Information (702) 597-7600
Admission with Taxes $44, includes dinner

Cast Size 35 (with 38 horses)

Nights of Lowest Attendance Monday and Tuesday

Usual Show Times 6 and 8:30 p.m.

Topless No

Author's Rating ★★★

Overall Appeal by Age Group

Under 21	21–37	38–50	51 and older
★★★★	★★★★	★★★★	★★★★

Duration of Presentation An hour and a half

Description and Comments *Tournament of Kings* is a retooled version of *King Arthur's Tournament.* The idea is that Arthur summons the kings of eight European countries to a sporting competition in honor of his son Christopher. Guests view the arena from dinner tables divided into sections; a king is designated to represent each section in the competition. Ladies-in-waiting and various court attendants double as cheerleaders, doing their best to whip the audience into a frenzy of cheering for their section's king.

Consumer Tips No matter where you sit, you're close to the action. The air-conditioning system is steroidal, so you might consider bringing a wrap. Seating is reserved, so you can walk in at the last minute and don't have to tip any greeters or seaters. Dinner is served without utensils and eaten with the hands, so you might want to wash up beforehand.

Comedy Clubs

There is a lot of stand-up comedy in Las Vegas, and several of the large production shows feature comedians as specialty acts. A comedy club is usually a smaller showroom with a simple stage and two to five stand-up comics. In most of the Las Vegas comedy showrooms, a new show with different comedians rotates in each week. There are four bona fide Las Vegas comedy clubs:

Harrah's	The Improv at Harrah's
Riviera	Comedy Club
Tropicana	Comedy Stop
Excalibur	Catch a Rising Star

There are two shows each night, seven days a week (except at the Riviera, where there are three performances on Friday and Saturday nights). The humor and audience at the comedy clubs tend to be young and irreverent. A favorite and affordable entertainment for locals as well as tourists, comedy clubs enjoy great popularity in Las Vegas.

Comedy Stop

Type of Show Stand-up comedy
Host Casino and Showroom Tropicana—Comedy Stop Showroom
Reservations and Information (702) 739-2714
Admission with Taxes $17.50 includes 2 drinks and gratuity
Cast Size Usually 3 comedians
Nights of Lowest Attendance Monday–Wednesday
Usual Show Times 8 p.m. (nonsmoking) and 10:30 p.m. (smoking)
Duration of Presentation An hour and a half

Description and Comments   To reach the Comedy Stop Showroom
take the elevator (between the main casino and the shopping arcade) up one
floor. After being seated, patrons trade their ticket stubs at a self-service bar
for two drinks. If you use the Trop's self-parking lot, allow an extra ten minutes to get to the showroom.

An Evening at the Improv

Type of Show Stand-up comedy
Host Casino and Showroom Harrah's—The Improv
Reservations and Information (702) 369-5111
Admission with Taxes $27.45
Cast Size 3–4 comedians
Nights of Lowest Attendance Wednesday and Thursday
Usual Show Times 8 and 10 p.m.   **Dark** Monday

Description and Comments   Drinks are not included, but there is a self-
serve cash bar. The showroom is on the second floor at the top of the escalator from the main casino. Reserved seats may be purchased by phone or in
person up to 30 days in advance.

Riviera Comedy Club

Type of Show Stand-up comedy
Host Casino and Showroom Riviera—Mardi Gras Showrooms, second floor
Reservations and Information (702) 794-9433
Admission with Taxes $21.95 general admission; $38.45 VIP (includes tax,
tip, and 2 drinks); weekend late-night shows of more risqué "Extreme
Comedy" are $16.50 and $24.75
Cast Size Approximately 4 comedians
Nights of Lowest Attendance Sunday–Wednesday
Usual Show Times 8 and 10 p.m.; also Friday and Saturday 11:45 p.m.
(sometimes cancelled)

Description and Comments   Show tickets can also be purchased as a package with the Riviera's buffet. The food with the show-dinner combo is a good deal for the money but is not exactly a culinary breakthrough. The buffet is fast and convenient, however, and there is usually plenty of time to eat between shows. Seating is by the maître d'. There is no table service. After you are seated, proceed to the bar and turn in your ticket stub for drinks. Drinks are included even with the dinner combos.

Catch a Rising Star

Type of Show   Stand-up comedy
Host Casino and Showroom   Excalibur—Catch A Rising Star Showroom
Reservations and Information   (702) 597-7600
Admission with Taxes $17
Cast Size   Usually 2 comedians
Nights of Lowest Attendance   Sunday and Tuesday
Usual Show Times   7:30 and 10 p.m. nightly
Duration of Presentation   About an hour

Description and Comments   There are usually only two comedians, but each performs for 40–45 minutes. Because the showroom is too large for a comedy club, you should arrive early on weekends to get a good seat. On weekdays, also due to the showroom size, *Catch a Rising Star* is a good bet if you decide at the last minute that you'd like to take in a show.

Las Vegas Nightlife

With the exception of patronizing comedy clubs, locals stay away from the Strip. Visitors, conversely, almost never leave it. Both groups miss some great nightlife.

Lounges and clubs are friendly citywide. Visitors can feel comfortable in places primarily frequented by locals, and vice versa. Profiled here alphabetically are the better nightspots.

Microbreweries, described in Part Five, Dining and Restaurants, are another off-Strip option.

BABY'S

Dance

Who Goes There: 21–29; college students

4455 Paradise Road (Hard Rock Hotel); (702) 693-5000   Strip Zone 1

What goes on After the last performance, The Joint showroom changes its attitude and caters to "Baby's." Male and female go-go dancers gyrate on stage as the dance floor fills with a young, hip crowd. Use valet or take a cab because parking at the Hard Rock can be limited on busy nights. The Hard Rock's main bar is also a happenin' place to meet new friends and watch the casino action.

The Beach

Dance music of the 1970s, 1980s, and 1990s

Who Goes There: 21–40+; locals, visitors, conventioneers (cosmopolitan mix)

365 Convention Center (corner of Paradise and Convention Center, across from the Convention Center); (702) 731-1925   Strip Zone 1

What goes on Singles, couples, and new friends alike dance, drink, eat, and laugh the night away in this "local's favorite" party club. Neon beer lights, palm fronds, coconuts, surfboards, and brightly painted murals give the club a beach flavor without adding salt or sand. Long lines begin at 9 p.m. and continue well past 2 a.m. on weekends.

Club Paradise

Upscale topless bar

Who Goes There: Men 21–65; professionals and conventioneers

4416 Paradise Road; (702) 734-7990   Strip Zone 1

What goes on Club Paradise is a very plush, upscale topless bar featuring more than 50 dancers in a setting designed to make executives feel at ease. Parking is valet only. Seating is by the maître d'. Though Club Paradise bills itself as a gentleman's club, women patrons are welcome.

Club Rio

Nightclub—Top 40 music

Who Goes There: 25–35 professionals; locals and visitors

3700 W. Flamingo (Rio Hotel); (702) 252-7777   Strip Zone 1

What goes on Sexy and stylish, Club Rio is the hottest nightclub for successful singles and the chic well-to-do. Arrive early to avoid the long lines after 11 p.m. The dress code encourages stylish attire (jackets for the men and dresses for the women).

Dylan's Saloon & Dance Hall

Recorded country music

Who Goes There: 25–50; urban and rodeo cowboys

4660 S. Boulder Highway; (702) 451-4006   Southeast Zone 5

What goes on   This dance hall has a spacious, 2,400-square-foot, silky smooth dance floor, two bars, friendly folks, and the usual rodeo decor. The party flows onto the patio and, on busy nights, the chain-linked, flood-lit, dirt area adjacent to the parking lot. Because the parking lot is quite dark in areas, women on their own are advised to ask for an escort to their car.

Gilley's Saloon, Dance Hall, and BBQ

Live country and rock and roll

Who Goes There: 21–55; real and urban cowboys, locals and tourists

3120 Las Vegas Boulevard S. (New Frontier); (702) 794-8200   Strip Zone 1

What goes on   The six-piece Gilley's All-Star Band starts at 9 p.m. Tuesday–Saturday; a deejay spins the tunes on Sunday and Monday. The smell of beer-battered onion rings, rotisserie chicken, and hickory-smoked pork permeates the place from the kitchen. The atmosphere is as heavily country as anywhere else in town—the heaviest on the Strip.

The Nightclub

Top 40/show combination

Who Goes There: 30–50; visitors, locals, conventioneers/ businesspeople

3000 Paradise Road (Las Vegas Hilton); (702) 732-5755 or (702) 732-5422
Strip Zone 1

What goes on   A combination of a Las Vegas showroom and a New York dance club, The Nightclub is a trendy art deco hot spot. On some nights a reserved ticket show is performed in the venue. At the conclusion of the show, the dance club cranks up. Dress is upscale yet casual.

Olympic Garden

Topless bar

Who Goes There: Men 21–65; locals, visitors, and conventioneers

1531 Las Vegas Boulevard S.; (702) 385-8987   Strip Zone 1

What goes on   It's not the classiest club in town, but it is one of the most relaxed and least aggressive. And the women are top of the line. At any given time, 50 of the most eye-popping strippers in varying degrees of undress are on display. Tuesday through Friday there's a male strip show on the second floor for local and visiting ladies (men must be accompanied by a woman).

Palomino Club

Totally nude dance club

Who Goes There: Men 21–65; tourists, locals, conventioneers

1848 Las Vegas Boulevard N.; (702) 642-2984   North Las Vegas Zone 4

What goes on   The Palomino offers both nude dancing and alcohol. Nine professionals and an equal number of so-called amateurs strip completely nude each night. A stand-up comic spells the dancers from time to time and provides the patrons with a good excuse to increase their alcohol consumption. For what it's worth, women are welcome.

Peppermill Inn's Fireside Lounge

Romantic and quiet

Who Goes There: 25–55; locals and tourists

2985 Las Vegas Boulevard S. (across from the Stardust, next to La Concha); Restaurant (702) 735-4177, Lounge (702) 735-7635   Strip Zone 1

What goes on   One doesn't expect a lounge like this in a 24-hour coffee shop. It's inviting, quiet, and even tranquil. Tropical greenery creates secluded alcoves of privacy. Drinks are a bit pricey and vary in quality depending on the bartender.

RA

Top 40, techno, and dance

Who Goes There: 21–35; locals and tourists, college students to professionals

3900 Las Vegas Boulevard S. (Luxor); (702) 262-4000   Strip Zone 1

What goes on   Ever wonder what the Egyptian sun god does after a hard day's work? He parties with the night-worshipping crowd until the wee hours of the morning. Lines are long by midnight, so arrive early or be prepared to wait (hotel guests can use the VIP line). Call ahead for special events such as cage dancing contests and 1980s nights.

Sand Dollar Blues Lounge

Rhythm and blues

Who Goes There: Bikers to yuppies

3355 Spring Mountain Road (at Polaris); (702) 871-6651
Southwest Zone 3

What goes on   Everyone from attorneys to bikers sits back for an evening full of moody and marvelous blues by popular Las Vegas or out-of-town bands. It's standing-room only on Friday, Saturday, and special-event nights. The club's unshaven appearance may deter some solo ladies from experiencing a night of great blues. The regulars make sure everything stays cool. The Sand Dollar is hard to spot at night, so arrive early or come by cab.

Studio 54

Dance, Top 40

Who Goes There: 25–40; locals, tourists, and trendy people

3799 Las Vegas Boulevard S. (MGM Grand); (702) 891-1111   Strip Zone 1

What goes on   If you love a club with an attitude then Studio 54 is for you. If you prefer a bit more fun and friendliness, try RA or Club Rio. Studio 54 is located at the Tropicana and Las Vegas Boulevard entrance—it's a long walk from both valet and the parking garages.

Tommy Rocker's Cantina and Grill

Top 40 and Jimmy Buffett–style music

Who Goes There: 25–30; professionals and career starters

4275 S. Industrial Boulevard; (702) 261-6688   Strip Zone 1

What goes on   Singles and couples gather to sing Jimmy Buffett songs, shoot a friendly game of pool, cheer their favorite team on the big-screen TV, or indulge in the tasty libations and food fare. Tommy Rocker's offers plenty of parking, friendly yet professional security, and a great attitude. The music is loud but not deafening, allowing for conversation. Come early for best seating.

VooDoo Cafe and Lounge

Restaurant and lounge with live entertainment

Who Goes There: 25+; upscale visitors and locals

3700 W. Flamingo Road, (Rio Hotel); (702) 252-7777, ext. 8090
Southwest Zone 3

What goes on Sweethearts, friends, and colleagues enjoy conversation, decent regional cuisine, and live music. The lounge crowd grows as the evening approaches midnight and the VooDoo Café diners and late-night party-goers ascend to the 51st floor (really the 41st floor). Music lovers relax and enjoy the jazz and blues beat in the lounge. Adventurous souls party on the open-air patio, amazed at the electrifying view of the famous Strip and the surrounding Las Vegas valley. After 10 p.m. on Friday and Saturday, expect a long line at the VooDoo elevators (managed by a humorless staff) and a very smoky lounge upstairs.

Las Vegas below the Belt

Don't Worry, Be Happy

Las Vegas exults in its permissiveness and makes every effort to give visitors freedom to have fun. Behind the hedonism, however, is a police department that works hard to make Las Vegas safe for visitors. In few other large cities could travelers carry large sums of money safely. The Strip and downtown, especially, are well patrolled, and most hotels have in-house security forces.

Police patrol downtown and the Strip in cars, on foot, and on mountain bikes, which allow quick pursuit of pickpockets or purse snatchers. Streets connecting the Strip with Paradise Road and the Las Vegas Convention Center are also safe. When tourists are robbed, they're usually far from downtown or the Strip, and often are trying to buy drugs.

Organized Crime and Cheating

Few visitors walk through a casino without wondering if the games are rigged or the place is owned by the mob. When legalized gambling was new, few people outside of organized crime had experience managing gaming operations. Hence, mob figures came to work in Nevada.

The formation of the Nevada Gaming Commission and the State Gaming Control Board as part of a government assault on organized crime purged the mob from Las Vegas. This ouster, plus the Nevada Corporate Gaming Acts of 1967 and 1969 (allowing publicly held corporations such as Hilton, Holiday Inn, Bally, and MGM to own casinos), at last brought respectability to Las Vegas gambling.

The limited cheating that exists in Las Vegas is usually perpetrated by gamblers, not the house, though honest players at the cheater's table may also get burned.

Skin Games—Sex in Las Vegas   Although nudity, prostitution, and pornography are tightly regulated in Las Vegas, the city offers a near-perfect environment for marketing sex. Over 50% of visitors are men, most between ages 21 and 59. Some come to party, and many, particularly conventiongoers, are lonely. Almost all have time and money on their hands.

Stripping on the Strip   Las Vegas is moving away from nudity and eroticism. "Girlie" (and "boy") shows are tame by many standards. In larger showrooms, this is an accommodation to the growing percentage of women in the audience. More often, however, it's the result of a city law that says you can offer totally nude entertainment or you can serve alcoholic beverages, not both.

Topless showgirls often merely embellish a production that features song, dance, and variety acts. Some shows offer both a topless and a "covered" performance.

Topless Bars   The main difference between a topless bar and a totally nude nightclub (aside from the alcohol regulations) is a G-string. Topless bars aren't inexpensive, but they're conveniently located, including Girls of Glitter Gulch on Fremont Street and Cheetah's at 2112 Western Avenue. We profile Palomino Club, Club Paradise, and Olympic Garden above.

How Felons Choose Their Victims

Felons choose their marks by observing a potential victim's attire and behavior. Wearing lots of jewelry and flaunting big bills are sure to attract attention. Stupid bets suggest inexperience, and excessive drinking lowers inhibitions and defenses. Playing without friends suggests you're a solitary business traveler or on vacation and perhaps hungry for companionship.

Beware of loners of either sex. If you meet somebody interesting, resist the urge to rush the relationship. Don't go anywhere to be alone. Don't tell anyone your room number. If you're traveling alone, don't say so.

Part Three

Gambling

The Way It Is

Gambling is the reason Las Vegas exists. It fuels the local economy, paves the roads, and gives the city its identity.

To tourists, gambling is a game. To those who earn their living from it, gambling is mathematics. The gambler *hopes* to win a fortune, but the casinos *know* that in the long run the fortune will belong to the house. The games, the odds, and the payoffs are carefully designed to ensure that outcome.

The casino does risk one bet: that it can entice enough people to play.

A casino costs millions of dollars, with a staff numbering in the hundreds. Before a nickel of profit is set aside, all the bills must be paid and the payroll met. Regardless of the house's overwhelming advantage at the tables, it cannot stay in business unless a lot of people come to play, and the larger the casino, the more gamblers are required.

Casinos compete aggressively and creatively to lure customers, offering low-cost buffets, dollar shrimp cocktails, stage shows, lounge entertainment, free drinks, gambling tournaments, and slot clubs. The most recent tactic is to package the casino itself as a tourist attraction. This explains the Mirage's erupting volcano in the front yard, white tigers in the entrance hall, and live sharks in the parlor.

The Short Run

If you ask a mathematician or a casino owner if you can win gambling in a casino, the truthful answer is yes, but only in the short run. The longer you play, the more certain it is that you will lose.

In casino games, patrons either do not understand what they are up against, or they understand but consider their losses a fair price to pay for an evening's entertainment.

Many unfortunate casino gamblers:

1. Don't understand that the game is biased against them.

2. Don't take their winnings and quit when they're ahead in the short run.

3. On losing, continue playing and redouble their efforts to pull even or win, ultimately (in the long run) compounding their losses.

A Little Restraint
While the casinos will not offer a fair game (like betting even money on the flip of a coin), they do understand that if they hammer you every time you come to play, sooner or later you will quit coming. Better to let you win every once in a while.

The Battle and the War
In casino gambling, the short run is like a battle, and either player or casino can win. However, the casino always wins the war. Players should stage commando raids: Get in, do some damage, and get out. Hanging around too long in the presence of superior force can be fatal.

Of course, it takes discipline to withdraw when you're winning, and it's even harder to call it quits when you're losing.

The House Advantage
If casinos engaged in fair bets, they'd win about half the bets and lose about half. This arrangement would be more equitable, but it wouldn't pay the casino's mortgage or foot the bill for pirate battles, bargain room rates, or $2 steaks.

To ensure sufficient income to meet their obligations and show a profit, casinos establish rules and payoffs for each game to give the house an advantage. There are three basic ways the house establishes its advantage:

I. Rules of the Game Are Tailored to the House's Advantage
In blackjack, for instance, the dealer by rule always plays his own

hand last. If any player busts (attains a point total over 21), the dealer wins by default without having to play out his hand.

2. The House Pays Off at Less Than the Actual Odds

Imagine a carnival wheel with ten numbers. When the wheel is spun, each number has an equal chance of coming up. If you bet a dollar on number six, there is a one-in-ten chance you will win and a nine-in-ten chance you will lose. Gamblers express odds by comparing the likelihood of losing to the likelihood of winning. In this case, nine chances to lose and one to win, or nine to one. If the game paid off at the correct odds, you would get $9 every time you won (plus the dollar you bet). Each time you lost, you would lose a dollar

But a casino can't play you even-up and still pay the bills. Therefore, if a casino owner installed a wheel with ten numbers, he would decrease the payoff. Instead of paying at the correct odds (nine to one), he might pay at eight to one. If you won on your last bet and were paid at eight to one, you would lose a dollar overall. Starting with $10, you lose your first nine bets (you're out $9) and on your last, winning bet you receive $8 and get to keep the dollar you bet. Having played ten times at the eight-to-one payoff, you have $9 left, for a total loss of $1. The house's advantage in this game is 10% (one-tenth).

The house advantage for actual casino games ranges from less than 1% for certain betting situations in blackjack to in excess of 27% on keno and some slots. Although 1% doesn't sound like much of an advantage, it will get you if you play long enough. Plus, it adds up for the house.

Because of variations in rules, the house advantage for a game in one casino may be greater than the house advantage for the same game in another casino. In most Las Vegas casinos, for instance, the house has a 5.26% advantage in roulette. At Sam's Town, however, because of the elimination of 00 (double zero) on certain roulette wheels, the house advantage is pared to about 2.7%.

Rule variations in blackjack swing the house advantage from almost zero in single-deck games to more than 6% in multiple-deck games with draconian rules.

The bottom line: blackjack (played competently), baccarat, and certain bets in craps minimize the house advantage and give the player the best opportunity to win. Keno and wheel of fortune are sucker games. Slots, video poker, and roulette are not much better.

The money you take to the table is your "bankroll." When wagering money from your winning bets, you are adding to your original stake. In gambling parlance, this is "action," and it's very different from bankroll. When you risk your winnings in additional betting, you give the house a crack at a much larger amount than your original stake.

HOUSE ADVANTAGES

Baccarat	1.17% on bank bets, 1.36% on player bets
Blackjack	0.5% to 5.9% for most games
Craps	1.4% to almost 17%, depending on the bet
Keno	20% to 35%
Roulette	5.26% to 7.89%, depending on the bet
Slots	2% to 25% (average 4% to 14%)
Video poker	1% to 12% (average 4% to 8%)
Wheel of Fortune	11% to 24%3.

3. The House Takes a Commission   In all casino poker games and in certain betting situations in table games, the house will collect a commission on a player's winnings.

Games of Chance and the Law of Averages
Casinos offer games of chance (roulette, craps, keno, bingo, wheel of fortune, slots, baccarat) and games of chance *and* skill (poker and blackjack).

In games of chance, coins flip or wheels spin, and what happens is what happens. A player can guess the outcome but cannot influence it. Games of chance operate according to the law of averages. If you flip a coin ten times, the law of averages leads you to expect that half of the tosses will come up heads and the other half tails. If a roulette wheel has 38 slots, the law of averages suggests the ball will fall into a particular slot one time in 38 spins.

The coin, the roulette ball, and the dice, however, have no memory. They just keep doing their thing. If I toss a coin, it has no obligation to keep to the law of averages. The operative word, it turns out, is "averages," not "law."

What the law of averages *does* say is that, *in percentage terms,* the more times you toss the coin, the closer you will come to approximating the predicted average.

Games of Chance and Skill

Blackjack and poker are games of chance and skill, meaning that the knowledge, experience, and skill of the player can influence the outcome. All avid poker or bridge players can recall when they played for hours without being dealt a good hand. That's the chance part. In order to win (especially in blackjack, where there's no bluffing), you need good cards.

If you're dealt something to work with, you can use your skill to try to make your good hand even better. In casino poker, players compete against each other the same way they do at Uncle Bert's back home. The difference is that, in the casino, the house takes a small percentage of each winning pot as compensation for hosting the game (are you listening, Uncle Bert?). Although not every casino poker player is an expert, your chances of coming up against an expert are good. Our advice on casino poker: If you aren't a tough fish, don't swim with the sharks.

Blackjack likewise combines chance and skill. In blackjack, however, players compete against the house (the dealer). Players have choices and options in blackjack, but the dealer's play is bound by rules.

Still, in blackjack, as in every casino game, it's ludicrous to suggest that the house is going to surrender its advantage.

Playing It Smart

Experienced, noncompulsive, recreational gamblers play in a disciplined and structured manner. They recommend:

1. Never Gamble when You're Tired, Depressed, or Sick   Limit drinking. Alcohol impairs judgment and lowers inhibitions.

2. Set a Limit before You Leave Home on How Much You're Willing to Lose Gambling   Do not exceed this limit.

3. Decide Which Game(s) Interests You, and Know the Rules before You Play   First-timers at craps or baccarat should take lessons (free at casinos). Virgin blackjack players should buy a good book and learn basic strategy. For all three, observe games in progress for an hour or more before buying in. Shun games like keno and wheel of fortune, in which the house advantage is overwhelming.

4. Decide How Long You Want to Play and Devise a Gambling Itinerary Consistent with Your Bankroll   For example, you'll be in Las Vegas two days and want to play about five hours each day. If you have $500 to gamble, that's $250 a day. Dividing that by five hours, you come up with $50 an hour.

Now, think of your gambling in terms of sessions instead of hours. You're going to play five sessions a day with $50 to wager at each.

5. Observe a Strategy for Winning and Losing   On buying in, place your session allocation by your left hand. Play your session money only once during a session. Any time you win, return your original bet to the session-allocation stack (left hand), and place your winnings by your right hand. Never play chips or coins you have won. When you have gone through your allocation once, pick up your winnings (right hand) and quit. The diVerence between your original allocation and what you walk away with is your net win or loss for the session.

During the session, bet consistently. If you're losing, don't up your bets in an eVort to get even.

If you doubled your allocated stake during a session (in this case, walked away with $100 or more), take everything in excess of $50 and put it aside as winnings, not to be touched for the remainder of your trip. If you won but didn't double your money, or if you had a net loss (less than $50 in your win stack), use this money in your next session.

6. Take a Break Between Sessions.

7. When You Complete the Number of Sessions Scheduled for the Day, Stop Gambling   Period.

THE INTELLIGENCE TEST

If you have been paying attention, here is what you should understand:

1. All gambling games favor the house, and the house will always win in the long run.

2. It costs a lot to build, staff, and operate casinos, and casinos must attract many players in order to pay the bills and make a profit.
3. Casinos compete fiercely and offer incentives ranging from 50-cent hot dogs to free guest rooms to attract the right customers.

Question:	Given the above, what customer gets the best deal?
Answer:	The person who takes advantage of all the incentives without gambling.
Question:	What kind of customer gets the next best deal?
Answer:	The customer who views gambling as recreation, gambles knowledgeably, bets sensibly, limits the amount he or she is prepared to wager, and enjoys all of the perks, but stays in control.
Question:	What customer gets the worst deal?
Answer:	The person who thinks he or she can win. This person will foot the bill for everyone else.

Gaming Instruction and Resources

Most casino games are fairly simple, once you know what's going on. We recommend you join the free gaming lessons offered by casinos. Friendly and fun, the lessons introduce you to both the rules and the etiquette of games. You learn to play and bet without wagering money. Many casinos offer low-minimum-bet "live games" after the instruction. Gamblers' nonplaying companions also would benefit from the lessons. Spectating is more interesting if you know what's going on.

When "new games" are added, casinos generally offer instruction for a limited time. The latest rages are Red Dog poker and, owing to increasing numbers of Asian gamblers, Pai Gow and Pai Gow poker.

Written References and the Gambler's Book Club   If you can't find references on casino gambling at your local library or bookstores, call the Gambler's Book Club at (800) 634-6243 for a free catalog. The club's Las Vegas store is at 630 South 11th Street; (382-7555). It stocks single issues of the *Las Vegas Advisor.*

Funbooks, Matchplay, and Understanding the Marquees

Casino games are full of jargon. Most terms are clear from context, but those below are common in ads and coupons, and on marquees, and confuse many people.

Crapless Craps   Dice totals of 2, 3, 11, and 12 count as point numbers.

Double Exposure 21   A version of blackjack in which both of the dealer's cards are dealt face up.

Double Odds   The option in craps of making an odds bet twice the size of your line bet.

Funbooks   Booklets of coupons free from some casinos. Usually included are coupons for souvenir gifts, discount show tickets, discount meals, two-for-one or free drinks, and matchplay (see below). Some funbooks offer exceptional value; others are a hustle. On balance, coupon books are worth checking out.

Loose Slots   Slot machines that are programmed to pay off more frequently. The term is usually applied to machines with a return rate of 94% or higher, meaning that the house advantage is 6% or less.

Matchplay Coupons   Coupons from funbooks or print ads that can be redeemed for matchplay chips. These must be combined with an equal amount of your money on certain table game bets. If you win, you're paid for the entire bet in real money. If you lose, the dealer takes both your money and the matchplay chips.

Megabucks Slots   A statewide progressive slot machine network with grand jackpots in excess of $3 million.

Single-Deck Blackjack   Blackjack dealt from a single deck as opposed to two or more decks shuffled together.

Triple Odds   The option in craps of making an odds bet three times the size of your line bet.

Where to Play

We receive a lot of mail from readers asking which casino has the loosest slots, the most favorable rules for blackjack, and the best odds on craps. We directed the questions to veteran gambler and tournament player Anthony Curtis, publisher of the *Las Vegas Advisor*. Here's his reply:

> *The best casino in Las Vegas to play blackjack, video poker, and other gambling games could be almost anyplace on a*

WHERE TO GO FOR LESSONS

Baccarat
Bally's
Caesars Palace
MGM Grand
Riviera

Blackjack
Bally's
Caesars Palace
Circus Circus
Excalibur
Harrah's
Lady Luck
Luxor
MGM Grand
Riviera
Sahara
Silverton
Stardust

Caribbean Stud
Harrah's
MGM Grand
Riviera
Stardust

Craps
Bally's
Caesars Palace
Circus Circus
Excalibur
Flamingo
Harrah's
Lady Luck
Luxor
MGM Grand
Riviera
Sahara
Sam's Town
Stardust

Let It Ride
Harrah's
MGM Grand
Riviera
Stardust

Pai Gow and Pai Gow Poker
Bally's
Caesars Palace

Harrah's
MGM Grand
Stardust

Poker
Monte Carlo

Roulette
Bally's
Caesars Palace
Circus Circus
Excalibur
Harrah's
Luxor
MGM Grand
Riviera
Stardust

Video Poker
Fiesta

given day due to spot promotions and changing management philosophies. A few casinos, however, have established reliable track records in specific areas. Absent a special promotion or change in policy, I recommend these casinos as the best places to play each of the games listed:

Blackjack: Slots A Fun   The only casino in Las Vegas dealing a single-deck game where the dealer stands on soft 17 and double down is allowed after splits. The combination results in a player advantage of .13% with perfect basic strategy.

Quarter Slots: Fitzgeralds   Competes hard for quarter slot players. Perhaps Las Vegas's best slot club.

Dollar Slots: Fiesta   Heavy-duty slot house. Good machine selection in the "Jackpot Blitz Zone." Periodic promo pays extra million dollars for hitting Megabucks there.

Craps: Binion's Horseshoe   Legendary dice house. Low minimums. Recently allowed up to 100x odds on $1 pass line bets.

Quarter Video Poker: Reserve   Best pay schedule available for on the floor. Several return more than 100%.

Dollar Video Poker: Reserve   More of the above. Also a good slot club with frequent multiple-point days.

Roulette: Monte Carlo   Single zero in the heart of the Strip. The absence of the usual double zero lowers the casino's edge from 5.26% to 2.7%.

Baccarat: Binion's Horseshoe   The mini-baccarat tables on the first floor charge a 4% commission on winning bank bets, compared to the standard 5%. This concession lowers the house edge from 1.06% to 0.6%.

Keno: Silverton   A comparison of keno return percentages shows casinos that target locals offer the best chance of winning.

Bingo: Showboat   Most elegant and airy bingo room in Las Vegas.

Poker: Bellagio   Biggest room and most action around the clock.

Race/Sports Betting: Caesars Palace   Big, bustling room covering all major events.

Let It Ride: O'Shea's   Consistent $3 minimum.

Caribbean Stud: Binion's Horseshoe   High reset on progressive with low minimums.

Pai Gow Poker: Desert Inn   Best rules in town. Player may bank every other hand.

Gambling Bug's Most Painful Bite

Some people can't handle gambling, just as some can't handle alcohol. The "high" described by the compulsive gambler parallels the experience of drug or alcohol abusers.

Compulsive gamblers attempt to use "the action" to cure for a variety of ills, much like some people use alcohol and drugs to lift them out of depression, anxiety, or boredom, and make them *feel* more in control. The compulsive gambler blames circumstances and other people for the suffering he causes.

If this sounds like you or someone you love, get help. In Las Vegas, Gamblers Anonymous meets almost every night. Call 385-7732. Gamblers Anonymous also is listed in your local white pages.

Slot Machines

Slot machines, including video poker, have eclipsed table games in popularity. Most casinos have allocated more than half of their floor space to slot machines. The popularity is easy to understand.

First, slots allow a person to gamble at at low or high stakes. Machines accept from a penny to $500 (special tokens). Quarter slots, however, are the most popular.

Second, many people like slots because no human interaction is required. A slot player can gamble and never speak to a soul.

Finally, slot machines appear to be simple. The only obvious thing you have to know is to put a coin in the slot and pull the handle. But there's more.

What You Need to Know before You Play Slot Machines

Basics: All slot machines have a slot for inserting coins, a handle to pull or button to push to activate the machine, a visual display where you can see reels spin and stop on each play, and a coin tray that winnings may drop into.

Most slot machines have three reels, but some have as many as eight. Each reel has some number of "stops," positions where the reel can come to rest. Reels with 20, 25, or 32 stops are the most common. On each reel at each stop is a single symbol (cherry, plum, orange, etc.). If three of the same symbol line up on the pay line when the reel stops spinning, you win.

Many machines also pay for single cherries in the far left or far right position, two cherries side by side, or two bells or two oranges side by side with a bar on the end.

Almost all machines accept more than one coin per play (usually three to five). No matter how many coins the machine will take, only one is required to play.

If you put in additional coins (bet more), you buy:

1. Payoff Schedules Posted above the reel display are payoff schedules that show how much you can increase your payoff (if you win) by playing extra coins. Usually the increase is straightforward. If you play two coins, you win twice as much as if you play one coin; three coins, three times as much; and so on. Some machines, however, have a grand jackpot that pays only if the maximum number of coins has been played. If you line up the symbols for the grand jackpot but haven't played the maximum number of coins, you won't win. Always read and understand a machine's payoff schedule before you play. If it isn't clear, ask an attendant or find a simpler machine.

2. Multiple Pay Lines When you play your first coin, you buy the pay line in the center of the display. By playing more coins, you buy additional pay lines. Each line you purchase gives you another way of winning. Make sure each line you buy is acknowledged by a light before you pull the handle.

Nonprogressive vs. Progressive Slot Machines Nonprogressive slot machines have fixed payoffs. How much you would get for each winning combination is posted on the machines.

Progressive slot machines have a grand jackpot that grows until somebody hits it. After that jackpot is won, a new one starts to grow. Individual machines can offer modest progressive jackpots, but the really big jackpots (several thousand to several million dollars) are possible only on machines linked to other machines. Sometimes an "island," "carousel," or "bank" of machines in a casino is linked to create a progressive system. The more these machines are played, the faster the jackpot grows. The largest progressive jackpots, however, come from multi-casino systems that may cover the state.

Progressives offer an opportunity to strike it rich, but they give fewer intermediate wins.

How Slot Machines Work

Almost all slot machines are controlled by microprocessors. This means machines can be programmed and are more like computers than mechanical devices. Each machine has a "random number generator" that we call a "black box." Each second, the black box spits out hundreds of numbers randomly selected from among about four billion available.

The numbers the black box selects trigger a set of symbols on the display, determining where the reels stop. Black boxes pump out numbers continuously, regardless of whether the machine is being played. If you are playing a machine, the black box will call up hundreds or thousands of numbers in the few seconds between plays while you sip your drink, put some money in the slot, and pull the handle.

There's no such thing as a machine that is "overdue to hit." Each spin of the reels is an independent event. The only way to hit a jackpot is to activate the machine at the exact moment the black box randomly selects a winning number.

Cherry, Cherry, Orange   The house advantage is known for every casino game except slots. With slots, the advantage is whatever the casino wants it to be. In Atlantic City, the maximum legal house advantage is 17%. There's no limit in Nevada. Interviews with former casino employees suggest, however, that the house advantage in Las Vegas ranges from about 2.5% to 25%, with most machines giving the house an edge of between 4% and 14%.

Casinos advertise their slots in terms of payout or return rate. If a casino says its slots return up to 97%, that means the house has a 3% advantage. We're skeptical when casinos advertise machines paying up to 98%. In most casinos, only a few slots will be programmed to return more than 92%.

Slot Quest   A slot machine that withholds only a small percentage of the money played is "loose," while a machine that keeps most of the coins it takes in is "tight." Because return rates vary among casinos and machines in a casino are programmed to withhold differing percentages of coins played, slot players devote much energy to finding the casinos with the loosest machines. There are several theories on how to pinpoint these casinos.

Some say smaller casinos such as Slots-A-Fun and Silver City, which compete against large neighbors, must program their slots to provide a higher return to players. Alternatively, some folks play slots only in casinos patronized predominantly by locals (Gold Coast, Palace Station, Boulder Station, Fiesta, Texas Station, El Cortez, Gold Spike, Showboat, Sam's Town, Arizona Charlie's, Santa Fe). They reason that these casinos vie for regular customers and must offer competitive win rates. Downtown casinos competing with the Strip are likewise cast in the "we try harder" role.

Machines in supermarkets, restaurants, convenience stores, airports, and lounges are purported to be very tight.

Within a casino, veteran slot players theorize, the loosest slots are by the door or in the waiting area outside the showroom. Loose machines here, the theory goes, demonstrate to passersby and show patrons that the house has loose slots.

Of the theories for finding loose machines in a specific casino, the one that makes the most sense is to select a casino and play there long enough to develop a relationship with the slot attendants. Be friendly. Engage them in pleasant conversation. If the casino has a slot club, join and use the club card so slot personnel will regard you as a regular. If the attendants are responsive and kind, and you win, tip them. After a couple of hours, the attendants will begin to take an interest in you. Ask them to point out a good (loose) machine. Tip them for the information and tip again if you do well on the machine. Don't blame them if you lose.

Maximizing Your Chances of Winning on the Slots In any multiple-coin slot machine, you're more likely to win if you play the maximum number of coins. If you want to bet only 25 cents per play, you will probably be better off putting five nickels into a multiple-coin nickel slot than one quarter into a multiple-coin quarter slot. Never play a progressive machine unless you bet the maximum number of coins. To do otherwise is to contribute to a jackpot you have no chance of winning.

Common Sense

If you line up a winner and nothing happens, don't leave the machine. Jackpots sometimes exceed the coin capacity of the machine and must be paid by the cashier. Call an attendant. While you wait, don't play further on the machine. When the attendant arrives, check his casino employee identification.

If the pay lines fail to illuminate when you're playing multiple coins, don't leave or activate the machine (pull the handle). Call an attendant.

Slot Clubs and Frequent-Player Clubs

Most casinos have slot or frequent-player clubs. Their purpose is to foster customer loyalty by providing incentives. You can join a club in person at some casinos or apply by mail. No dues are charged. You receive a plastic membership card. This is inserted into certain quarter and dollar slots (including video poker machines). When your card is in the receptacle, you are credited for the action you give that machine.

Programs vary, but generally you are awarded "points" based on how long you play and how much you wager. Some clubs award points for both slot and table play. Accumulated points can be redeemed for awards ranging from casino logo apparel to discounts (or comps) on meals, shows, and rooms.

If you enjoy gambling all around town, you may never accrue enough points in one casino to earn a prize. Nonetheless, it's a good idea to sign up. Joining gets you on the casino's mailing list. You'll be offered discounts on rooms and other deals. Frequent business travelers should join their hotel's slot club.

Video Poker

Never in casino gambling has a new game become so popular so quickly. All across Nevada, casinos are reallocating game-table and slot space to video poker machines.

In video poker, you aren't playing against anyone (no professional gamblers!). Rather, you're trying to make the best possible five-card-draw poker hand. On the most common machine, you insert your coin(s) and push a button marked "deal." Your original five cards are displayed on a screen. Below the screen and under each card pictured are "hold" buttons. After evaluating your hand and planning strategy, you designate the cards you want to keep by pressing the appropriate hold button(s). If you hit the wrong button or change your mind, most machines have an "error" or "erase" button, allowing you to revise your choices. When you press the hold button, the word "hold" will appear over or under that card on the display. Double-check the screen to make certain the cards you intend to hold are marked before you draw. If you don't want to draw any cards (you like your hand as dealt), press all five hold buttons.

When you're ready, press the button marked "draw" (on many machines, the same button as the deal button). Cards not held will be replaced. As in live draw poker, the five cards you have after the draw are your final hand. If the hand is a winner (a pair of jacks or better on most quarter or dollar machines), you will be credited the appropriate winnings on a meter. Retrieve these winnings by pressing the "cash-out" button and removing the coins from the tray. If you leave your winnings on the meter, you may use them to bet, eliminating the need to insert coins.

Winning hands and their respective payoffs are posted on or above the video display. As with other slots, you increase your payoffs and become eligible for jackpots by playing the maximum number of coins.

Both progressive and nonprogressive quarter and dollar video poker machines are available. Nonprogressives pay more on a full house (nine coins) and a flush (six coins) than progressives do (eight and five, respectively). Progressives feature a grand jackpot that builds until somebody hits it. Nonprogressives usually offer a bonus jackpot for a royal flush when the maximum coins are played.

Video poker machines are labeled according to these payoffs as "nine/six" or "eight/five" machines. Never play a progressive machine unless you're playing the maximum number of coins. By playing fewer than the maximum, you disqualify yourself for the grand jackpot. Plus, the return rate is lower than on a non-progressives. The jackpot on a nonprogressive can sometimes exceed that of a progressive.

In addition to standard draw poker, games with jokers or deuces wild are also available. Jokers wild machines normally pay on a pair of kings or better, while deuces wild pays on three-of-a-kind and up. Casinos clean up on wild card machines because few players understand the strategy of play.

With flawless play, the house advantage on nine/six quarter and dollar machines ranges up from about ½% (0.5%), and for eight/five machines and wild card programs, from about 3%. On nickel machines, the advantage is about 5–10%.

Table Games

All casino games in which you interact with casino personnel or other players are called "table games." These include blackjack, craps, Wheel of Fortune, roulette, baccarat, poker, Let It Ride, Caribbean stud, Pai Gow poker, and even keno and bingo: everything, in other words, except slots and other machines played by a single individual. The rules for all of these games vary from casino to casino. Some games (Wheel of Fortune, craps, baccarat) are purely games of chance, while others like blackjack and poker involve subtlety and skill. All table games are operated under the supervision of a casino employee, usually called a dealer (sometimes even when there's no dealing involved).

If you want to play one of the table games, we suggest availing yourself of the free lessons provided at most casinos.

Any game that appeals to you is all right if you're playing just for fun and pretty much expect to lose your money anyway. If, however, you want to give yourself a sporting chance of winning a little, you're well advised to limit your play to the games where the house has the smallest edge. These games are blackjack, baccarat, and pass line bets in craps. Blackjack is a simple game, but has many variations, and requires some skill. Baccarat and the pass line bets in craps do not require skill. Simply place your bet and the dealer will do the rest. Wheel of Fortune and keno are sucker games and should be avoided. All the other games fall somewhere in-between.

Almost all table games require some minimum bet, so choose a table where the minimum is affordable. Also take a minute or so before buying in to observe the dealer. Is he or she personable and friendly? If the dealer has an attitude, so should you: Find another table. Players at table games are routinely offered free drinks. This is part of the casino scene and does not obligate you in any way, except that it's considered good form to tip the waitress when your drink arrives.

For card games keep your hands above the table, and for all games, do not touch your bet once play in underway except as the rules of the game allow. Always feel absolutely free to quit whenever you want, or to switch tables.

Part Four

Shopping and Seeing the Sights

Shopping in Las Vegas

The most interesting and diversified specialty shopping in Las Vegas is centered at the Fashion Show Mall on the Strip. The Forum Shops at Caesars Palace, and the Grand Canal Shoppes at the Venetian. These three venues, within walking distance of each other, collectively offer the most unique concentration of upscale retailers in the United States. The Forum Shops and the Grand Canal Shoppes are not your average shopping centers. In fact, both are attractions in their own right. Fashion Show Mall, by comparison, is plain but with a great lineup of big-name department stores.

At the intersection of Las Vegas Boulevard and Spring Mountain Road, the Fashion Show Mall is anchored by Saks Fifth Avenue, May Company, Neiman Marcus, Macy's, Nordstrom, Bloomingdale's, Lord & Taylor, and Dillard's, and contains 144 specialty shops, including four art galleries. The theme here: Shopping is king. The Fashion Show Mall is the place to go for that new sport coat, tie, blouse, or skirt at a reasonable price.

The Forum Shops, situated between Caesars Palace and the Mirage, offers a Roman market–themed shopping environment. Approximately 100 shops and restaurants line an ancient Roman street punctuated by plazas and fountains. Though indoors, clouds, sky, and celestial bodies are projected on the vaulted ceilings to simulate the actual time of day outside. A new west wing features an IMAX 3-D simulator attraction called *Race For Atlantis.*

The Grand Canal Shoppes' setting is the modern-day canals of Venice. Sixty-five shops, boutiques, restaurants, and cafes are arrayed along a quarter-mile-long Venetian street flanking a canal. Gondolas navigating the canal add a heightened sense of commerce and activity. The centerpiece of the Grand Canal Shoppes is a replica of St. Mark's Square.

The new Aladdin includes a 450,000-square-foot shopping and entertainment complex called Desert Passage. The venue recreates street scenes from real and imaginary North African and eastern Mediterranean towns. Like the Grand Canal Shoppes, Desert Passage offers primarily upscale boutique shopping, but more of it, with 144 shops and restaurants compared to the Canal Shoppes' 65.

At Paris is Rue de la Paix—31,000 square feet of upscale French boutique shopping. Another Strip shopping venue is the Showcase, adjacent to the MGM Grand.

There are two large neighborhood malls in Las Vegas, the Boulevard Mall and the Meadows. The Boulevard Mall, with 122 stores anchored by Sears, JC Penney, Marshalls, Dillard's, and Macy's, is on Maryland Avenue, between Desert Inn Road and Flamingo Road. The Meadows, featuring the same department stores (except for Marshalls), offers 73 stores spread over two levels. The Meadows is situated between West Charleston Boulevard and the Las Vegas Expressway (US 95) on Valley View.

A large discount shopping venue has materialized about five miles south of Tropicana Avenue on Las Vegas Boulevard near the Blue Diamond Road exit off I-15. A mile or so south of Blue Diamond Road on Las Vegas Boulevard is the Vegas Pointe Plaza, with a total of 50 factory-direct shops. Just north of Blue Diamond Road is a Belz Factory Outlet Mall with 155 stores. The easiest way to reach the outlets is to drive south on I-15 to Exit 33, Blue Diamond Road. Proceed east on Blue Diamond to the intersection with Las Vegas Boulevard. Turn left on Las Vegas Boulevard to the Belz mall, or right to the Vegas Pointe Plaza.

About an hour southwest on I-15 in Primm, Nevada, is Fashion Outlet Mall, offering themed dining and 100 outlet stores. You'll find Williams-Sonoma, Pottery Barn, Versace, Brooks Brothers, Calvin Klein, and Last Call from Neiman Marcus, among others.

Unique Shopping Opportunities

Wine & Liquor   Our favorite store for liquor and a decent bot-
tle of wine is Town Pump Liquors, with five locations: 953 East
Sahara Avenue, 735-8515; 6040 West Sahara Avenue, 876-
6615; 1725 E. Warm Springs Road, 897-9463; and 4410 W.
Craig Road, 645-9700.

Art   Look for galleries in the Fashion Show Mall, The Forum
Shops, and the Grand Canal Shoppes.

Gambling Stuff   If you are in the market for a roulette wheel,
a blackjack table, or some personalized chips, try the Gamblers
General Store at 800 South Main, (702) 382-9903, or (800)
322-CHIP outside Nevada. For books and periodicals on gambling, we recommend the Gamblers Book Club store near the
intersection of South 11th Street and East Charleston, (702)
382-7555. If you have always wanted a slot machine for your living room, you can buy one at Showcase Slot Machines, 4305
South Industrial Road, (702) 740-5722.

Head Rugs   The largest wig and hairpiece retailer in the United
States is in Las Vegas. At 953 East Sahara Avenue, Serge's Showgirl Wigs inventories over 7,000 hairpieces and wigs. Call (702)
732-1015.

Zoot Suits   Vintage Apparel & Collectibles is at the corner of
South 6th Street and Charleston. If you only want to zoot up for
a special occasion, rentals are available. Call (702) 383-9555.

Baseball Cards   Smokey's Sports Cards is open seven days a
week. Smokey's is at 3734 Las Vegas Boulevard South (the
Strip), (702) 739-0003, **www.smokeys.com.**

Seeing the Sights

Not a gambler? Don't worry. Las Vegas dishes up a smorgasbord
of attractions and amusements for all ages.

MGM Grand Attractions

In 1999, the MGM Grand opened a tri-story 5345-square-foot
lion habitat that houses up to five of the big cats. The lions are
on duty from 11 a.m. until 11 p.m. daily and admission is free.

Mandalay Bay Attractions

The Shark Reef aquarium features sharks, rays, sea turtles, and dozens of other denizens of the deep in a 1.3 million gallon tank. If you don't like fish, separate exhibits showcase rare golden crocodiles and pythons. Something for everybody you might say. The Shark reef audio tour is open daily from 10 a.m. until 11 p.m. Admission is about $14 for adults and $10 for children 12 and under. Call (702) 632-4555 for more information.

Adventuredome at Circus Circus

Adventuredome is designed to resemble a classic Western desert canyon. Set among the rock structures and 90-foot waterfall are a roller coaster, a flume ride, an inverter ride, and Chaos, a spinning amusement. There are also some rides for small children. Embellishing the scene are several life-sized animatronic dinosaurs, a re-creation of an archeological dig, a fossil wall, and a replica of a Pueblo Indian cliff dwelling. The premier attractions are the Canyon Blaster corkscrew roller coaster; and the Rim Runner, water flume ride. Guests can reach the theme park by proceeding through the rear of the main casino to the entrance and ticket plaza situated on the mezzanine level. For exact admission prices on the day of your visit, call (702) 794-3939.

Bellagio Attractions

The big draw at the Bellagio was the Gallery of Fine Art Exhibition, displaying works by Cézanne, van Gogh, and other notables. In 2000, MGM-Grand acquired the Bellagio, promptly closed the art gallery, and sold off most of the art. The gallery reopened in 2001 and now hosts traveling exhibitions. Open 10 a.m. through 10 p.m. daily, most exhibitions runs about $12. Reservations are recommended on weekends. Call (702) 693-7722 for ticket information.

Bellagio's free outdoor spectacle is a choreographed fountain show, which uses 1,200 fountains that blast streams of water as high as 200 feet. Almost 5,000 white lights and musical accompaniment by Sinatra, Pavarotti, and Strauss, among others, complete the picture.

Luxor Attractions

The Luxor offers two paid attractions inside the pyramid on the level above the casino. *In Search of the Obelisk* (in the Egyptian ruins) consists of two motion simulators: A runaway freight elevator and a runaway tour tram. The second attraction, a seven-story IMAX 3-D theater with a 15,000-watt sound system runs 24 hours a day and costs about $8.50.

Las Vegas Hilton Attractions

Star Trek: The Experience is a 16-minute "experience" that culminates in a four-minute space flight simulation ride. Besides a museum, the ride, and a gift shop, *Star Trek: The Experience* includes an electronic games arcade, a restaurant, and a lounge. The overall experience earns *Star Trek* a first-place ranking among Las Vegas's simulator attractions. The best times to see *Star Trek: The Experience* are on weekdays from 12:30 to 2 p.m. or after 4 p.m. It's open 11 a.m. to 11 p.m. daily. Admission is $24.99, including tax ($19.99 for Nevada residents, children and seniors). *Hint:* the entrance from "Deep Space Promenade" is free. For information call (702) 732-5111 or (888) GO-BOLDLY.

Stratosphere Attractions

The Stratosphere Tower stands 1,149 feet tall and offers an unparalleled view of Las Vegas, 24 hours a day. At night, the dark desert circumscribes a blazing strand of twinkling neon. A 12-level pod crowns the futuristic contours of three immense buttresses that form the tower's base. Level 12, the highest level, serves as the boarding area for the High Roller, a roller coaster, and the Big Shot, an acceleration/free-fall thrill ride. An outdoor observation deck is situated on Level 9, with an indoor observation deck directly beneath it on Level 8. Level 7 features a 220-seat lounge, and Level 6 houses an upscale revolving restaurant. Levels 4 and 3 contain meeting rooms. The view from the tower is so magnificent that we recommend experiencing it at different times of the day and night.

The rides are a mixed bag. Where the High Roller is hype at best, the Big Shot is cardiac arrest. Sixteen people at a time are seated at the base of the skyward projecting needle that tops the pod. The next thing you know, you are blasted 160 feet straight up in the air at 45 miles per hour and then allowed to partially free fall back down.

The elevators to the tower are at the end of the shopping arcade on the second floor of the Stratosphere, above the casino.

Tickets for the tower can be purchased at the elevator lobby (on the second floor) or at various places in the casino. The ticket line at the elevator lobby is usually shorter. Tower tickets cost about $11, including rides. Expect big crowds at the tower on weekends. If you must see the tower on a weekend, go in the morning as soon as the tower opens.

Another way to see the tower without a long wait is to make a reservation for the Top of the World restaurant. To be safe, reservations should be made at least two weeks in advance. When you arrive, inform the greeter in the elevator lobby that you have a dinner reservation and give him your confirmation number. You will be ushered immediately into an express elevator. The restaurant is pricey, but the food is good and the view is a knockout, and you do not have to pay the $6 tower admission. Most folks dress up to eat at the Top of the World.

Tower hours are Sunday–Thursday, 10 a.m.–1 a.m., and Friday and Saturday, 10 a.m.–2 a.m. For more information call (702) 380-7777.

Caesars Palace Attractions

So detailed is Caesars Magical Empire dining and entertainment complex that you could visit several times without exhausting its surprises.

In 1998, Caesars launched Race for Atlantis, an IMAX 3-D, simulator experience at The Forum Shops. The IMAX visuals are well done, but the story line is muddled and not very compelling. The entrance is oV the rotunda at the far west end of The Forum Shops. Go before or during a show at the rotunda's Fountain of the Gods. Queues are longest just after a fountain show.

Also at the Forum Shops is the 3-D Cinema Ride, a simulator attraction featuring a haunted graveyard, space flight, and submarine race. Other attractions at Caesars include the Omnimax Theater, off the casino, where documentaries are projected onto a six-story screen. IMAX admission is $7 for adults and $5 for children ages 2 to 12. Race for Atlantis costs $9.50 for adults and $6.75 for juniors (under 42 inches tall). Hours are 10 a.m. to 10 p.m. daily.

Mirage and Treasure Island Attractions

Mirage and Treasure Island attractions are top quality—and free. The two biggies are Treasure Island's pirate battle and the Mirage's erupting volcano. The pirate battle occurs, weather permitting, every 90 minutes from 4 to 10 p.m. (11:30 p.m. on Fridays and Saturdays in warmer months). As you face Treasure Island, the pirate ship is on your left and the British man-of-war enters from the right. The best vantage points are on the rope rail facing the man-of-war. On weekdays, claim your spot 15–20 minutes before show time; weekends, 35–45 minutes. You can see almost everything by joining the crowd at the last minute. If you're short or have children in your party, arrive early and stand by the rail.

The Mirage's volcano erupts every 15 minutes between 8 p.m. (6 p.m. in winter) and midnight, weather and winds permitting. Because shows are frequent, getting a rail-side vantage point isn't diYcult. If you want to combine the volcano with a meal, grab a window table in the second-floor coVee shop of the Casino Royale across the street.

The Mirage displays some of Siegfried and Roy's white tigers inside its entrance (free). A nice dolphin exhibit is open from 11 a.m. to 5:30 p.m. weekdays and 10 a.m. to 5:30 p.m. weekends ($10; ages 10 and younger free). For information, call Mirage at (702) 791-7111 or Treasure Island at (702) 894-7111.

Paris Las Vegas Attractions

A little more than half the size of the original, the big draw at Paris is the 540-foot-tall replica of the Eiffel Tower. It costs a stiff nine bucks to ride up, but you must first queue up to buy tickets. Your ticket will show a designated time to report to the escalator If you're late you'll be turned away and there are no refunds. The escalator will deposit you in another line where you'll wait for the elevator. The elevators run from 10 a.m. until 1 a.m. except when it's raining. Though all this hopping from line to line is supposed to take 5 to 20 minutes, we found 40 to 60 minutes more the norm. If accessing the observation platform seems like too much work, take the separate elevator that serves the restaurant and bar on the 11th floor of the tower. You don't need reservations to patronize the bar, but you must be nicely dressed. Jackets are recommended for men—absolutely no jeans, T-shirts, tank tops, or sandals. The bar is open nightly from 5 p.m. until midnight.

Sahara Attractions

The Speedworld simulator ride at the Sahara was inspired by Indy car racing. You can drive a race car in an interactive simulated race or strap in as a passenger for a 3-D movie race. Interactive race cars respond exactly like real cars to braking, acceleration, and steering. You can even choose between manual or automatic (recommended) transmission. Your eight-minute race pits you against other drivers. During the race, driving at high speed demands intense concentration. Visuals projected in front of your car are good but come at numbing speed. If you're motion-sensitive, the simulator will make your stomach spin.

Race once to understand how everything works. After that, it's more enjoyable, and you can be more competitive. Start on a simple course. After each race, you'll receive a computer-generated report on your performance. Each race you drive costs $8; the 3-D movie costs $3. Rides cost about $8 each, but for exact prices, call (702) 737-2111 on the day you go.

Venetian Attractions

The Venetian is host to the first Madame Tussaud's Wax Museum in the United States. Covering two floors and 28,000 square feet, the museum is about half the size of the original London exhibit. Approximately 100 wax figures are displayed in theme settings. The museum is open daily at 10 a.m. Admission is about $13.

A Word about Strip Roller Coasters

There are now four roller coasters on the Strip. After careful sampling, we have decided that, although shorter, the Canyon Blaster at Adventuredome offers a better ride than the more visually appealing Manhattan Express at New York–New York. Speed lives up to its name, but is overpriced at $8. The other coaster, the High Roller at the Stratosphere is a dud.

Free Stuff

The eye-popping Fremont Street Experience electric light show is produced on a four-block-long canopy over the Fremont

Street pedestrian concourse downtown. Shows begin at dusk and run about once an hour through 11 p.m. on weekdays and midnight on weekends. Masquerade in the Sky, a musical Mardi Gras parade suspended from a track in the ceiling, circles the Rio's casino. The water and laser show at Sam's Town, starring animatronic animals and choreographed fountains, is staged four times daily. All three shows are free. Outdoor productions at Bellagio, Treasure Island, and the Mirage are also free.

Really Expensive Thrills

If you're really flush, you can fly an authentic World War II fighter. Cost is $190–590 for 15 minutes to an hour at North American TopGun at the Boulder City Airport. For information call (702) 294-8778. For $99 and up you can go about the same speed a foot off the ground at the Richard Petty Driving Experience. The Driving Experience is located at the Las Vegas Motor Speedway. Call (702) 643-4343 for additional information.

Other Area Attractions

If you have children, try the **Scandia Family Fun Center** (phone (702) 364-0070) for miniature golf and the **Lied Discovery Museum** (phone (702) 382-5437) for an afternoon of exploration and education. Across the street from the Lied is the **Las Vegas Natural History Museum** (phone (702) 384-3466). The **Wet 'n Wild** water theme park (phone (702) 737-3819) may be the best place in Las Vegas for teens and is also good for preschoolers.

Adults should check out the **Auto Collection at the Imperial Palace** (phone (702) 731-3311) where more than 200 antique vehicles are on display. Part of a much larger collection, these automobiles are rotated periodically to keep the exhibit fresh. Seeing the collection is well worth the admission price of $6.95, $3 for seniors and children under 12, though discount coupons are readily available in the local visitor guides and at the Imperial Palace casino. **The Liberace Foundation and Museum** (phone (702) 798-5595) on East Tropicana Avenue is one of Las Vegas's most popular tourist attractions. Housed in multiple buildings connected by a parking lot, the exhibit chronicles the music, life, and excesses of Liberace. Adjacent to the MGM Grand is the **Showcase,** a shopping, dining, and entertainment venue.

Natural Attractions near Las Vegas

The hour-and-a-half trip from the banks of Lake Mead to the high ponderosa forests of Mount Charleston encompasses as much environmental change as driving from Mexico to Alaska.

Red Rock Canyon, the Valley of Fire, the Mojave Desert, and the Black Canyon of the Colorado River are world-class scenic attractions. In combination with the Spring Mountains' wet summits, they comprise one of the most dramatically diversified natural areas in North America.

Hoover Dam

Definitely worth seeing, Hoover Dam offers a film, guided tour, and theater presentation—all well done. Arrive by 9 a.m. Monday, Thursday, or Friday, and do the tour first. After 9:30, long lines form, especially Tuesdays, Wednesdays, Saturdays, and Sundays. There's little advantage taking a bus tour to the dam. You still must wait in line for presentations.

Part Five

Dining and Restaurants

Dining in Las Vegas

In an effort to attract customers in an increasingly competitive market, casino owners have literally scoured the country for famous, big name restaurants, convincing the proprietors to open a branch in Las Vegas. Michael Mina (Aqua) has opened NOB-HILL, replacing Gatsby's at MGM Grand. Wolfgang Puck has added Cili at the posh Bali Hai Golf Club, which is open to the public on the strip. Delmonico Steak House was imported from New Orleans; Spago and Pinot from Los Angeles; Morton's from Chicago, and the list goes on and on.Celebrity chefs such as Julian Serrano (Picasso at the Bellagio) and Maurizio Mazzon (Canaletto at the Venetian), arriving with the regularity of Swiss trains, have opened scores of additional new restaurants. There's also been a proliferation of brew pubs, seven at last count.

Subsidized Dining
and the Free-Market Economy

There are two kinds of restaurants in Las Vegas: those that are an integral part of a hotel-casino, and those that must make it on the merits of their food. Celebrity-run restaurants and gourmet rooms in the hotels are usually associated with the casinos. Their mission is to pamper customers who are giving the house gambling action. Many of the folks in a hotel restaurant are dining as guests of the casino. If you are a paying customer in the same restaurant, the astronomical prices you are charged help subsidize the feeding of all the comped guests.

Restaurants independent of casinos work at a considerable disadvantage. Successful proprietary restaurants in Las Vegas

must offer something very distinct and very good at a competitive price. Their offer must be compelling enough to induce you
to travel to their location, forsaking the convenience of dining
in your hotel.

All of this works to the consumer's advantage, of course. High
rollers get comped in the gourmet rooms. Folks of more modest
means can select from among the amazing steak, lobster, and
prime rib deals offered by the casinos, or enjoy exceptional food at
bargain prices at independent restaurants. People with hardly any
money at all can gorge themselves on loss-leader buffets.

So Many Restaurants, So Little Time

Dining options have been shaped by the marketing strategies of
the casinos. While there are hundreds of restaurants in Las
Vegas, you will be able to sample only a handful during your
stay. But which ones? Our objective in this section is to point
you to specific restaurants that meet your requirements in terms
of quality, price, location, and environment.

Buffets

Buffets, used by the casinos to lure customers, have become a Las
Vegas institution. The majority of casinos operate their buffets
at close to cost or at a slight loss. A few casinos, mostly those
with a more captive clientele (like the Las Vegas Hilton, the
Mirage, and Caesars Palace), and the new breed of upscale
spreads (Bellagio, Paris) probably make money on their buffets.

Almost all of the buffets serve breakfast, lunch, and dinner,
changing their menus every day. Prices for breakfast range from
under $4 to $10. Lunch goes for $6 to $14, with dinner ranging
between $7 and $27. At breakfast there is not much difference
between one buffet and the next (exceptions are at the Orleans,
Paris, and Bellagio). When it comes to lunch and dinner, however, some buffets do a significantly better job than others.

If you are looking for upscale gourmet-quality food and a large
variety to choose from, head straight for our top four buffets. If
you're hankering for well-seasoned meats and vegetables, ethnic
variety, and culinary activity, the other six will suffice nicely.

Our top choice of Las Vegas buffets is Sam's Town Firelight
Buffet. The buffet room is gorgeous and well laid-out. The quan-
tity, variety, and quality, of the selections are top-notch, and best
of all, the prices, especially for lunch, are extremely reasonable.

BUFFET SPEAK	
Action Format	Food cooked to order in full view of the patrons
Gluttony	A Las Vegas buffet tradition that carries no moral stigma
Groaning Board	Synonym for a buffet; a table so full that it groans
Island	Individual serving area for a particular cuisine or specialty (salad island, dessert island, Mexican island, etc.)
Shovelizer	Diner who prefers quantity over quality
Fork Lift	A device used to remove shovelizers
Sneeze Guards	The glass/plastic barriers between you and the food

Sam's Town, Aladdin, Paris, Rio, Fiesta, Texas and Sunset Stations, Main Street Station, Reserve, Harrah's, Paris, Orleans, and Bellagio all have the new-style "superbuffets." Aladdin includes an excellent Middle Eastern station, the only one in town. The Fiesta buffet has a monster rotisserie for barbecuing every kind of flesh known to man and Las Vegas's first and only coffee bar. Texas Station introduced a chili bar with nine selections and cooked-to-order fajitas; it also has good barbecue, Chinese, Italian, and lots of pizza. Paris has a made-to-order crepe station. Bellagio is the most expensive superbuffet—and is worth every penny. Seafood galore, gourmet entrées, perfect vegetables—this joint has it all. For the money, we like lunch here better than dinner. Main Street Station is the only superbuffet downtown, served in one of the most aesthetically pleasing buffet rooms in town. The buffet room at The Regent Las Vegas is also stunning and has a great view to boot. Main Street's cuisine has a distinct Hawaiian emphasis, which is where most of its patrons come from. The Reserve has wood-fired pizza, a Mongolian grill, and a daily seafood island. The Mirage Buffet is the Strip's version of the good Golden Nugget Buffet downtown. It opens at 3 p.m. and is uncrowded until about 5:30 p.m. Harrah's buffet gets an A for effort, a B for quality, and a C for value. Mandalay Bay's buffet is expensive and odd; it's small, congested, and slow. But Treasure Island, Palace and Boulder Stations, MGM Grand, and Luxor are tried-and-true; you won't go wrong at any of these. The different buffet stations at Paris represent different regions of France, and the dining room has several intimate dining nooks and a view as well. The buffets at the Rio, Fiesta, Regent Las Vegas, Orleans, and Texas, Palace, Sunset and Boulder Stations are the favorites of Las Vegas locals.

A number of casinos have very acceptable, though not exceptional, buffets. Not worth a special trip if you are staying or playing elsewhere, these buffets are just fine if you happen to be at the hotel in question when you get the urge to go to the trough.

LAS VEGAS'S TEN BEST BUFFETS		
Buffet	Quality Rating	Last Year's Ranking
1. Sam's Town Firelight Buffet	98	not ranked
2. Aladdin Spice Market Buffet	98	not ranked
3. Bellagio Buffet	97	1
4. Paris Le Village Buffet	95	not ranked
5. Rio Carnival World Buffet	93	9
6. Reserve Grand Safari Buffet	92	4
7. Orleans French Market Buffet	91	6
8. Main Street Station Garden Court Buffet	90	3
9. Fiesta Festival Buffet	89	5
10. Sunset Station The Feast	85	10

Seafood Buffets

Several casinos feature seafood buffets on Friday and sometimes on other days. The best of the seafood buffets are the Rio's Village Seafood Buffet and The Flamingo's Paradise Garden (both daily), Fiesta's seafood night (Wednesday), and the Fremont's Seafood Fantasy (Wednesday and Friday).

The Rio's seafood buffet is the most expensive buffet, but the quality and variety of this piscatory repast are unbelievable, including small lobster tails (dinner), peel-and-eat shrimp, Dungeness crab legs, Manila steamers, and oysters on the half-shell;

seafood salads, and chowders. Rio's dessert selection is out-standing.

The Flamingo began serving all-you-can-eat cold king crab legs, cold steamed clams and mussles, and several seafood entrées in early 2000. At the Fiesta's Wednesday night seafood buffet, you can gorge on all the steamed and fried clams, mussels, oysters, snow crab legs, peel-and-eat shrimp, seafood gumbo, and baked, stir-fried, broiled, grilled, and wokked fish you can cram in. The Fremont's Wednesday and Friday Seafood Fantasy isn't quite as extensive or expensive as the Fiesta's, but its quality and popular-ity are almost as strong.

Buffet Line Strategy

Popular buffets develop long lines. The best way to avoid the crowds is to go Sunday through Thursday and get in line before 6 p.m. or after 9 p.m. If you go to a buffet on a weekend, arrive extra early or extra late. If a large trade show or convention is in town, you will be better off any day hitting the buffets of casinos that do not do a big convention business. Good choices among the highly ranked buffets include Texas Station, Fiesta, Main Street Station, Palace Station, Boulder Station, Silverton, Show-boat, the Fremont, and Reserve.

Some restaurants now use pagers to let diners know when their table is available. This gives you a bit more freedom to roam around while you wait, but many pagers have a fairly small range. Even better, you'll never wait for a table at Paris' buffet. You check in and they'll tell you a specific time to return to be seated—and they usually peg it dead on the money.

Champagne Brunches

Upscale, expensive Sunday champagne brunches with reserved tables, imported champagne, sushi, and seafood are making an impact on the local brunch scene. Although there are a plethora of value-priced champagne brunches, the big-ticket feasts at-tract diners who are happy to pay a higher tab for fancy food and service and reservations to avoid a wait. Reservations are ac-cepted at all of the following.

■ **Sterling Brunch,** Bally's Steakhouse   (702) 739-4111
   At $69.95 per person (plus tax) it's the most costly, but there's no shortage of diners who love it. The lavish selection of foods includes a host of breakfast items, freshly made sushi, real

lobster salad, caviar, and French champagne. Pheasant and rack of lamb appear regularly. The dessert selection is awesome. Available: 9:30 a.m.–2:30 p.m.; reservations are required.

- **Grand Champagne Brunch at the Brown Derby,** MGM Grand (702) 891-3110 (after 9 a.m.)
  A complete seafood bar, filet mignon, prime rib, and rack of lamb are regular features. There are more than 50 items and desserts. Adults, $39.95 per person (plus tax); children ages 5–12, $19.95; children under age 5 dine free. Available: 9 a.m.–2:30 p.m.

- **The Steak House,** Circus Circus (702) 734-0410
  Featured are many breakfast items, steak and seafood, entrées, and salads. Adults, $21.95 (all-inclusive); children ages 6–12, $10.95. Three seatings: 9:30 a.m., 11:30 a.m., and 1:30 p.m.

- **Gospel Brunch,** House of Blues, Mandalay Bay (702) 632-7777
  "Praise the Lord and pass the biscuits!" This is the most raucous and joyous Sunday brunch in town. The food is soulful as well as the music: fried chicken, skillet cornbread, jambalaya, turnip greens, and banana bread pudding. Adults, $32.95; children ages 7–11, $16.95. Two seatings at 10 a.m. and 1 p.m.

- **Garduno's Margarita Brunch,** Fiesta Hotel (702) 631-7000
  Colorful decor, margaritas galore, and strolling mariachis make for happy dining. An omelet station, fajita station, peel and eat shrimp, crab legs, and fresh oysters as well as 15 or more Mexican specialties. Come early or prepare to wait. Adults, $11.99 per person; children ages 3–8, $8.99. Available: 10 a.m.–3 p.m.

Other good brunches include Caesars Palace (which often features Bananas Foster), the Fiesta (serving Mexican specialties and substituting margaritas for champagne to correspond with the southwest theme), Bellagio, and Golden Nugget.

Meal-Deals

In addition to buffets, many casinos offer special dining deals. While the meal-deals generally deliver what they promise in the way of an entrée, many of the extras that contribute to a quality dining experience are missing. With a couple of notable exceptions, the specials are served in big, bustling restaurants with the atmosphere of a high school cafeteria.

Our biggest complaint, however, concerns the lack of attention paid to the meal as a whole. We have had nice pieces of meat served with tired, droopy salads, stale bread, mealy microwaved potatoes, and unseasoned canned vegetables.Finally, at the odd times these meals are offered it's hard to take advantage of many of the specials.

To stay abreast of special dinner offerings, your best bet is to subscribe to the *Las Vegas Advisor,* a monthly newsletter that provides independent, critical evaluations of meal-deals. To subscribe call (800) 244-2224, or pick up the latest edition, at the Gamblers Book Club store at 630 South 11th Street, (702) 382-7555.

Steak   Our favorite is the 16-ounce porterhouse steak dinner at the Redwood Bar & Grill in the California, (702) 385-1222. A complete steak dinner can be had for about $13, excluding drinks, taxes, and tips. This special does not appear on the menu. Just ask for it. Other deals: There's a great 16-ounce T-bone served in the coffee shop of the Gold Coast 24 hours a day for $7.95, (702) 367-7111. Little Ellis Island, attached to the Super 8 motel on Koval Lane near East Flamingo Road, serves an excellent $4.95 steak dinner. It's not on the menu, so you have to ask for it. The Hard Rock Hotel has a steak and shrimp special in the coffee shop for $5.95, (702) 693-5000.

Prime Rib   One of the best prime rib specials is available at the San Remo's Ristorante del Flori coffee shop, (702) 739-9000. They offer a generous piece of meat, accompanied by good sides. Downtown, the Lady Luck has a good prime rib special for $8–12, available 4–10 p.m. in the coffee shop, (702) 477-3000. Up the block at the California, you can get the smaller cut of meat during the same hours for $5.95. For $5 or $6 more you can dine at Sir Galahad's at the Excalibur, (702) 597-7777. The prime rib is excellent. Another good prime rib and crab leg special, is at Bally's ($12.50), (702) 739-4111. Jerry's Nuggett on Las Vegas Boulevard in North Las Vegas has a trio of prime rib meal deals for $8.95, $12.50, and $23, (702) 399-3000.

Lobster and Crab Legs Pasta Pirate at the California serves the best all-around shellfish specials, (702) 385-1222. Unfortunately, they are on-again, off-again. An excellent crab special for $14.95 is routinely offered in the Mediterranean Room at the Gold Coast, (702) 367-7111. Another good one is the king crab and steak special served for $18.95 at Roberta's at El Cortez, (702) 385-5200. The perennial favorite of the steak and lobster deals is found at Island Paradise Café at the Stardust ($9.95), (702) 732-6111. *Beware:* buffet lobsters chew like rubber.

Shrimp Cocktails The best and cheapest shrimp cocktails can be found at the Golden Gate, a small downtown casino. Other contenders are the Four Queens, Arizona Charlie's, and the Lady Luck.

Pasta and Pizza The Pasta Palace at Palace Station regularly runs half-price specials on excellent pasta entrées, and the Pasta Pirate at the California offers some of the best designer pasta dishes in town. The best play is to hit up pizza "satellite" outlets (fast-food counters attached to the Italian restaurants) at Boulder Station and Sunset Station for a quickie slice. You can also get a good slice of New York–style pizza at Toscana's at the Rio.

Breakfast Specials Our favorite breakfast deal is the huge ham and eggs special at the Gold Coast. One of the best breakfasts you will ever eat. Other worthwhile breakfast deals: steak and eggs at the Frontier, Arizona Charlie's, and the San Remo (24 hours); the ham and eggs breakfast at the Horseshoe (4 a.m.–2 p.m.); and the breakfast buffets at Regent Las Vegas and The Orleans.

New Restaurants

In 2001, the Brennan family opened a **Commander's Palace** at the Aladdin. This is New Orleans at it's best, and we sincerely hope the Sunday brunch here becomes a tradition to equal that of it's eastern kin. New York's **Blue Note** will also open a new eponymous restaurant at the Aladdin—and we're certain the food will be top notch.

In a different take on old names opening new restaurants, Aureole's Charlie Palmer has opened **Charlie Palmer Steak** with the Four Seasons. We have exceedingly high expectations.

Although no longer with the restaurant, Nicholas Nickolas (founder of Nick's Fishmarket) has opened **Bones,** a rib joint, at the former site of the Vito's Italian in the Orleans hotel.

The Cheesecake Factory has opened a new concept restaurant, **Café Lux,** at the Venetian. The concept? Big menu, reasonable prices, and fine cheesecake.

The Restaurants

Our Favorite Las Vegas Restaurants

We have developed detailed profiles for the best restaurants in town. Each profile features an easily scanned heading that allows you, in just a second, to check out the restaurant's name, cuisine, Star Rating, cost, Quality Rating, and Value Rating.

Star Rating   The Star Rating is an overall rating of the entire dining experience, including style, service, and ambience plus taste, presentation, and quality of food. Only the best receive five stars, the highest rating. Four-star restaurants are exceptional, and three-star restaurants are above average. Two-star restaurants are good. One star denotes an average restaurant with capability in some area—for example, an otherwise forgettable place with great barbecued chicken.

Cost   The expense notation indicates the cost of complete meal: entrée with vegetable or side dish, and choice of soup or salad. Appetizers, desserts, drinks, and tips are excluded.

Inexpensive $14 and less per person
Moderate $15–30 per person
Expensive More than $30 per person

Quality Rating   On the far right of each heading are a number and letter. The number is a Quality Rating based on a scale of 0–100, with 100 being the highest (best) rating. The Quality Rating is based on taste, freshness of ingredients, preparation, presentation, and creativity of food. Price is no consideration. If you want the best food and cost is no issue, look no further than the Quality Rating.

Value Rating   If, however, you look for both quality and value, check the Value Rating, expressed in letters:

A   Exceptional value, a real bargain
B   Good value
C   Fair value, you get what you pay for
D   Somewhat overpriced
F   Significantly overpriced

Location   Just below the address is a zone name and number.
The zone gives an idea of where the restaurant is. The zones we
use are (maps on pages 6–11):

Zone 1   The Strip and Environs
Zone 2   Downtown
Zone 3   Southwest Las Vegas
Zone 4   North Las Vegas
Zone 5   Southeast Las Vegas and the Boulder Highway

If, for example, you're staying downtown and intend to walk
to dinner, consider a restaurant in Zone 2.

Other Information   If you like what you see at first glance,
read the rest of the profile for details.

The Best Las Vegas Restaurants

Restaurants open and close all the time in Las Vegas. Our list is
confined to establishments with a proven track record over a
fairly long period. Newer restaurants (and older restaurants
under new management) are listed but not profiled. Our list is
highly selective. Excluding a restaurant doesn't mean it isn't
good, only that it wasn't among the best in its genre. Some
restaurants appear in more than one category.

THE BEST LAS VEGAS RESTAURANTS

Name	Star Rating	Price Rating	Quality Rating	Value Rating
Adventures in Dining				
Emeril's (New Orleans)	★★★★½	Very Exp	95	B
8-0-8 (Hawaiian/French)	★★★★	Expensive	93	C+
Marrakech (Moroccan)	★★★	Moderate	86	B

American

Aureole	★★★★★	Expensive	98	C
Spago	★★★★★	Mod/Exp	96	C
Olives	★★★★	Mod/Exp	95	B
Neros	★★★★	Expensive	90	C
Brown Derby	★★★★	Mod/Exp	87	C
Range Steakhouse	★★★½	Expensive	93	B
Hugo's Cellar	★★★½	Expensive	89	B
Redwood Bar & Grill	★★★½	Moderate	89	A
Grape Street	★★★½	Inexp/Mod	87	A
Red Square	★★★½	Expensive	87	C
Rainforest Café	★★★½	Moderate	86	B
Lawry's The Prime Rib	★★★½	Expensive	85	C
Magnolia Room	★★★½	Moderate	85	A
Top of the World	★★★½	Expensive	85	C
Wolfgang Puck Café	★★★½	Moderate	85	B
Wild Sage	★★★	Mod/Exp	89	B
Harley-Davidson Café	★★★	Moderate	85	C+
Kathy's Southern Cooking	★★★	Inexp/Mod	85	A

Asian/Pacific Rim

Malibu Chan	★★★★	Mod/Exp	90	C
China Grill	★★★★	Mod/Exp	89	B

Barbecue

Sam Woo Bar-B-Q	★★★	Inexpensive	89	A

Brazilian

Samba Grill	★★★★	Moderate	90	A
Rumjungle	★★★½	Mod/Exp	87	C

Brewpub

Barley's	★★★	Inexpensive	86	A
Triple Seven Brewpub†	★★★	Inexp/Mod	85	A

California-Continental

Drai's	★★★★½	Expensive	96	B

Chinese
   (see also Dim Sum)

Fortunes	★★★★	Mod/Exp	93	C+
Noodles	★★★½	Moderate	93	B
Peking Market	★★★½	Moderate	87	B
Chang	★★★	Moderate	85	B
Chungking East	★★	Inexpensive	85	A

Chinese/French

Mayflower Cuisinier	★★★★½	Mod/Exp	94	B
Chinois	★★★★	Mod/Exp	96	A

† No Profile

THE BEST LAS VEGAS RESTAURANTS (continued)				
Name	Star Rating	Price Rating	Quality Rating	Value Rating
Continental/French				
Picasso	★★★★★	Expensive	98	C
Renoir	★★★★★	Very Exp	98	C
Napa	★★★★★	Expensive	95	C
Buccaneer Bay Club	★★★★½	Mod/Exp	96	B
Andre's	★★★★½	Expensive	90	C
Fiore	★★★★	Mod/Exp	95	C
Michael's	★★★★	Very Exp	93	D
Mon Ami Gabi	★★★★	Mod/Exp	90	B
Seasons	★★★★	Very Exp	90	D
Isis	★★★½	Expensive	90	C
Pinot Brasserie	★★★½	Mod/Exp	89	C
Swiss Café	★★★½	Moderate	89	B
Café Nicolle	★★★½	Moderate	88	B
Pamplemousse	★★★½	Expensive	87	C
Burgundy Room	★★★½	Mod/Exp	85	B
Creole/Cajun				
Commander's Palace	★★★★	Expensive	90	C
Voodoo Café and Lounge	★★★½	Mod/Exp	85	C+
Cuban				
Florida Café	★★★½	Inexp/Mod	85	A
Dim Sum (see also Chinese)				
Chang	★★★	Moderate	85	B
Mirage Noodle Kitchen†	★★★	Moderate	85	B
Eclectic				
Cheesecake Factory	★★★½	Moderate	89	A
Greek				
Magnolia Room	★★★½	Moderate	85	A
Tony's Greco Roman†	★★★	Moderate	81	B
Indian				
Shalimar	★★★½	Mod/Exp	86	C
Italian				
Terrazza	★★★★½	Expensive	95	C+
Piero's	★★★★½	Expensive	92	C
Stefano's	★★★★	Mod/Exp	94	C
Trattoria del Lupo	★★★★	Mod/Exp	91	B+

† No Profile

THE BEST LAS VEGAS RESTAURANTS (continued)

Name	Star Rating	Price Rating	Quality Rating	Value Rating
Italian (continued)				
Antonio's	★★★★	Mod/Exp	90	B
Manhattan	★★★½	Mod/Exp	92	B
Ristorante Italiano	★★★½	Expensive	91	C
Mortoni's	★★★½	Mod/Exp	90	B
Anna Bella	★★★½	Inexp/Mod	89	A
Bootlegger	★★★½	Moderate	89	A
Ferraro's	★★★½	Mod/Exp	89	C
North Beach Café	★★★½	Moderate	89	A
Sazio	★★★½	Moderate	89	A
Bertolini's	★★★½	Moderate	88	B
Olio	★★★½	Mod/Exp	88	C
Fellini's	★★★½	Mod/Exp	87	A
Venetian	★★★½	Mod/Exp	87	B
Circo (Osteria Del)	★★★½	Mod/Exp	86	B
Magnolia Room	★★★½	Moderate	85	A
Il Fornaio	★★★	Mod/Exp	87	B
Japanese (see also Sushi)				
Shintaro†	★★★★	Mod/Exp	94	B+
Noodles	★★★½	Moderate	93	B+
Tokyo	★★★½	Moderate	85	B
Fuji	★★★	Inexp/Mod	84	B
Latin American				
Bohemias	★★★½	Moderate	89	B+
Lobster				
Alan Alberts	★★★½	Expensive	89	C+
Lobster House†	★★★½	Expensive	89	C+
Rosewood Grille	★★★½	Expensive	88	C+
Mediterranean				
Olives	★★★★	Mod/Exp	95	B
Mexican/Southwestern				
Coyote Café	★★★★	Mod/Exp	90	B
Garduno's Chili Packing Co.	★★★½	Inexp/Mod	89	B
Star Canyon	★★★½	Mod/Exp	89	B
Viva Mercado's	★★★½	Moderate	86	A
Ricardo's	★★★½	Moderate	85	B
Lindo Michoacan	★★★	Moderate	84	A

† No Profile

THE BEST LAS VEGAS RESTAURANTS (continued)

Name	Star Rating	Price Rating	Quality Rating	Value Rating
Middle Eastern				
Habib's	★★★½	Moderate	88	C
Haifa (Kosher)†	★★★	Moderate	85	B
Jerusalem (Kosher)	★★½	Inexp/Mod	80	B
Moroccan				
Marrakech	★★★	Moderate	86	B
Persian				
Habib's	★★★½	Moderate	88	C
Prime Rib				
Sir Galahad's	★★★½	Moderate	89	A
Redwood Bar & Grill	★★★½	Moderate	89	A
Lawry's The Prime Rib	★★★½	Expensive	85	C
Seafood				
Aqua	★★★★★	Expensive	98	C
Buzios	★★★★	Expensive	93	B
Kokomo's	★★★★	Expensive	93	C
The Tillerman	★★★½	Mod/Exp	87	C
Pasta Pirate	★★★½	Moderate	86	A
The Broiler	★★★	Moderate	85	A
Steak				
Prime	★★★★½	Expensive	96	C
Delmonico	★★★★	Very Exp	95	C
Ruth's Chris Steak House	★★★★	Expensive	94	C
Kokomo's	★★★★	Expensive	93	C
Samba Grill	★★★★	Moderate	90	A
The Palm	★★★★	Very Exp	85	C
Alan Alberts	★★★½	Expensive	89	C+
Morton's	★★★½	Very Exp	89	C
Redwood Bar & Grill	★★★½	Moderate	89	A
Rosewood Grille	★★★½	Expensive	88	C+
The Steak House	★★★½	Moderate	86	B
Billy Bob's Steakhouse	★★★	Mod/Exp	88	B
Yolie's †	★★★	Moderate	86	B
The Broiler	★★★	Moderate	85	A
Binion's Ranch Steakhouse	★★★	Moderate	82	B

† No Profile

THE BEST LAS VEGAS RESTAURANTS (continued)

Name	Star Rating	Price Rating	Quality Rating	Value Rating
Sushi (see also Japanese)				
Chinois	★★★★	Mod/Exp	96	A
Makino Sushi Restaurant	★★★★	Inexp/Mod	95	A
Teru Sushi	★★★½	Mod/Exp	89	C
Tokyo	★★★½	Moderate	85	B
Hamada of Japan †	★★★	Mod/Exp	84	C
Thai				
Lotus of Siam	★★★½	Mod/Exp	95	A
Noodles	★★★½	Moderate	93	B+
Vietnamese				
Noodles	★★★½	Moderate	93	B+
Pho Chien	★★★½	Inexp/Mod	89	A
Rooms with a View				
Eiffel Tower Restaurant †	★★★★	Very Exp	93	C
Top of the World	★★★½	Expensive	85	C
VooDoo Café and Lounge	★★★½	Mod/Exp	85	C+

More Recommendations

The Best Bagels

Bagel Oasis   9134 West Sahara Avenue, (702) 363-0811. The best bagels in town, New York–style; baked fresh daily; large selection.

Harrie's Bagelmania   855 E. Twain Avenue (at Swenson), (702) 369-3322. Baked on the premises; garlic and onion among the choices.

The Best Bakeries

Albina's Italian Bakery   3035 East Tropicana Avenue in the Wal-Mart Center, (702) 433-5400. Classic Italian pastries; baba au rhum, with and without custard; Italian and American cheesecakes; wide variety of cookies.

Great Buns   3270 East Tropicana Avenue (at Pecos), (702) 898-0311. Commercial and retail; fragrant rosemary bread, sticky buns, and apple loaf are good choices.

† No Profile

Tintoretto at The Venetian, Italian Bakery Canal Shops at the Venetian Hotel, (702) 414-3400. International breads, cakes, and cookies. Charming European design and a patio perfect for people-watching.

The Best Brewpubs

Barley's Casino and Brewing Company 4500 East Sunset Road, Suite 30, Henderson, (702) 458-2739. Reminiscent of old Las Vegas, Barley's features a small casino, attractive decor, and comfort foods galore.

Gordon Biersch Brewpub 3987 Paradise Road (Hughes Center) (702) 312-5247. Upbeat brewery restaurant with contemporary menu and surprisingly good food at reasonable prices.

Holy Cow! 2423 Las Vegas Boulevard, South (702) 732-2697. A trilevel barn-styled bar with comical cow decor. They also feature 24-hour food service.

Monte Carlo Pub & Brewery Monte Carlo (702) 730-7777. Located adjacent to the pool area in a faux-warehouse setting, this new brewpub offers six different beers and affordable food options. The beer is brewed right on the premises. Eighteen different pizzas are available, as well as sandwiches, pastas, and more.

Triple Seven Brewpub 200 North Main Street (Main Street-Station) (702) 387-1896. Late-night happy hour with bargain brews and food specials. Open 24 hours.

The Best Burgers

Kilroy's 210 South Buffalo Dr. (at West Charleston) (702) 363-4933 Half-pound burgers, choice of 15 toppings.

Lone Star
1290 East Flamingo Road (702) 893-0348
1611 South Decatur Boulevard (702) 259-0105
210 Nellis Boulevard (702) 453-7827
3131 North Rainbow (702) 656-7125
Cheese, Bubba, Texas, Mexi, or Willie half-pounders on a toasted onion bun.

Champagne Café   3557 South Maryland Parkway (702) 737-1699. Classic half-pounder with creative toppings.

Tommy's Hamburgers   2635 East Tropicana Avenue (702) 458-2533. Good eat-in or carry-out burgers.

The Best Delis

Bagelmania   855 East Twain (at Swenson) (702) 369-3322

Breakfast and lunch only. Full service bagel bakery and deli. On Tuesdays buy bagels by the dozen at half price.

Samuel's Deli   2744 North Green Valley Parkway, Henderson (702) 454-0565. Full-service deli, bakery, and restaurant. Home cooking and giant matzo balls.

Siena Deli   2250 East Tropicana Avenue (at Eastern) (702) 736-8424. Italian spoken here: everything Italian and home-made. Excellent bread baked fresh every morning. Siena bakes bread for many of the area's Italian restaurants.

Stage Deli   The Forum Shops at Caesars (702) 893-4045. Las Vegas branch of New York's famous pastrami palace; enormous menu runs gamut of Jewish specialties, including triple-decker sandwiches named for celebrities, and 26 desserts. Open wide—the sandwiches are skyscrapers.

The Best Espresso & Dessert

Café Nicolle   4760 West Sahara Avenue Suite 17 (at Decatur) (702) 870-7675   Sidewalk café west; cooling mist in summer.

Café Sensations   4350 East Sunset Road (east of Green Valley Parkway) (702) 456-7803. Scrumptious variety of baked goods, casual food, sandwiches, salads.

Coffee Pub   2800 West Sahara Avenue Suite 2A (702) 367-1913 Great breakfast and lunch location, imaginative menu.

Jitters Gourmet Coffee

2457 East Tropicana Avenue (at Eastern) (702) 898-0056,
2295 North Green Valley Parkway (702) 434-3112
8441 West Lake Mead Boulevard (702) 256-1902

Many varieties of coffees; homemade muffins; sandwiches, brownies, truffles. Popular local hangout.

La Piazza   Caesars Palace (702) 731-7110. Caesars' bakers create pies, cakes, and cookies to eat in or take out.

Spago   The Forum Shops at Caesars (702) 369-6300. Wolfgang Puck's pastry chef creates imaginative and sinful creations. Available all day in the café and at dinner in the dining room.

Starbucks Coffee Houses   Many area locations.

Tintoretto at The Venetian   Canal Shops at The Venetian, (702) 414-3400

Palio   Bellagio, (702) 693-8160. Cafeteria-style coffee house with scrumptious pastries and casual eats—quiche, salads, and sandwiches.

The Best Oyster & Clam Bars
Buzios   Rio (702) 252-7697
Oyster stews, cioppino, shellfish, and pan roasts. Table service or oyster bar.

Emeril's   MGM Grand (702) 891-1111

The Best Pizza
Bootlegger   7700 South Las Vegas Boulevard (702) 736-4939
Great selection; crispy, tender, homemade crust.

California Pizza Kitchen   Mirage (702) 791-7111
Trendy—even offers low-cal versions without cheese. No take-out service.

Metro Pizza   1395 East Tropicana Avenue (702) 736-1955
Fast service, generous with the cheese. Try the Old New York with thick-sliced mozzarella, plum tomatoes, and basil. Thick Ragu-style tomato sauce topping.

Spago   The Forum Shops at Caesars (702) 369-6300
Wolfgang Puck's regular specials include spicy shrimp, duck sausage, and smoked salmon with dill cream and golden caviar. Other toppings change frequently.

Venetian   3713 West Sahara Avenue (702) 876-4190
Old-time Las Vegas favorite; pizza with greens and olive oil (no cheese) is a popular item.

The Best Soup & Salad Bars

Paradise Garden Café   Flamingo Hilton (702) 733-3111
A good display at lunch; a large choice of seafood added at dinner.

Souper Salad   2051 North Rainbow (702) 631-2604
4022 South Maryland Parkway (702) 792-8555. Moderate prices, many combinations, shiny clean, and inexpensive.

Restaurants with a View

Circo   Bellagio, (702) 693-8150
Circo (Osteria Del) is adjacent to its pricier sister, Le Cirque. Tuscan fare with a view of Lake Como and Paris' Eiffel tower.

Eiffel Tower Restaurant   Paris (702) 948-6937
Fancy French food in a drop-dead gorgeous setting that towers over the strip. This is one spectacular view.

Picasso   Bellagio (702) 693-7223
Highly original food and glorious original artwork by Picasso. As good as it gets (since you can't eat in the Louvre!).

VooDoo   Rio Hotel and Casino (702) 252-7777
At the top of the new Rio tower, VooDoo offers the mystique of New Orleans, a complete view of the city, Cajun/Creole cooking, and late-night lounge.

Restaurant Profiles

Alan Alberts   ★★★ ½

Steak/Lobster   Expensive

Epicenter Plaza, North of the MGM Grand; (702) 740-4421
Strip   Zone 1

Dinner: Every day, 5–11:30 p.m.

Comments: Tucked away in the corner of a strip mall, Alan Alberts is a pleasant surprise. Lobsters are fairly priced—portions are generous.

Andre's   ★★★★ ½

Continental/French   Expensive

(Andre's continued)
401 S. 6th St.; (702) 385-5016
Downtown   Zone 2
Monte Carlo Hotel; (702) 798-7151
Strip   Zone 1

Dinner: Monday–Saturday, 6–9:30 p.m.

Comments: Owner-chef Andre Rochat is mostly in the kitchen of the Monte Carlo and makes frequent forays into the dining room.

Anna Bella   ★★★ ½

Italian   Inexpensive/Moderate

3310 South Sandhill Rd. at Desert Inn Rd.; (702) 434-2537
Southeast   Zone 5

Dinner: Tuesday–Sunday, 4:30–10 p.m.

Comments: Daily specials allow the chef to offer seasonal seafood and higher-end Italian dishes. Service can be slow at times, but be patient.

Antonio's   ★★★★

Italian   Moderate/Expensive

Rio, 3700 W. Flamingo Rd.; (702) 252-7777
Strip   Zone 1

Dinner: Friday–Tuesday, 5–11 p.m. Closed Wednesday and Thursday.

Comments: A fruity olive oil for dunking is offered instead of butter—the imported breadsticks are habit-forming; a complimentary liqueur is offered "to thank you for dining at Antonio's."

Aqua   ★★★★★

Seafood   Expensive

Bellagio; (702) 693-7223
Strip   Zone 1

Dinner: Every day, 5:30–11 p.m.

Comments: Raves for service, food, and decor. It's not easy to get a reservation if you're not staying at Bellagio, but it's worth any effort.

Aureole   ★★★★★

American   Expensive

Mandalay Bay; (702) 632-7401
Strip   Zone 1

Dinner: Every day, 6–11 p.m. lounge open (serving food) 5 p.m–1 a.m.

Comments: The wine tower is unique—the bottles are accessed by
black-clad females who hoist themselves up to the various levels to
remove the bottles.

Barley's   ★★★

Brewpub   Inexpensive

Town Center, 4500 E. Sunset, Green Valley; (702) 458-2739
Southeast   Zone 5

Hours: Brewer's Café: Sunday–Thursday, 7 a.m.–10 p.m.; Friday and
Saturday, 7 a.m.–11 p.m.

Comments: Generous amounts of food for the money. Entrées
include endless trips to the small soup and salad bar; it costs an
additional $2.95 with sandwiches and other items.

Bertolini's   ★★★ ½

Italian   Moderate

The Forum Shops at Caesars Palace; (702) 735-4663
Strip   Zone 1

Lunch & dinner: Sunday–Thursday, 11 a.m.–midnight; Friday and
Saturday, 11 a.m.–1 a.m.

Comments: The Sidewalk Café outside Bertolini's overlooks the
Forum's bustling scene and the Roman fountain. It's an ideal spot for
photos.

Billy Bob's Steakhouse & Saloon   ★★★

Steak   Moderate/Expensive

Sam's Town, Boulder Highway; (702) 456-7777
Southeast   Zone 5

Dinner: Sunday–Thursday, 5–10 p.m.; Friday and Saturday, 5–11 p.m.

(Billy Bob's Steakhouse & Saloon continued)

Comments: Prepare to eat as if you were heading out for a day on the range. The setting and the prices make Billy Bob's a popular choice.

Binion's Ranch Steakhouse ★★★

Steak   Moderate

Binion's Horseshoe Hotel; (702) 382-1600
Downtown   Zone 2

Dinner: Every day, 6–10:30 p.m.

Comments: The late Benny Binion believed in good food and large portions. The restaurant maintains his philosophy. One of the best buys in town.

Bohemias ★★★½

Latin American   Moderate

2550 Rainbow; (702) 253-6274
Zone 3

Dinner: Sunday–Thursday, 4–10 p.m.; Friday & Saturday, 4–11 p.m.

Comments: Have a pisco Rita or a mojitos or a caipirinha, the Brazilian sensation made with cachaca. These heady Latin cocktails liven up any meal.

Bootlegger ★★★½

Italian   Moderate

7700 S. Las Vegas Blvd.; (702) 736-4939
Strip   Zone 1

Lunch & Dinner: Tuesday–Friday, 11 a.m.–11 p.m.; Saturday and Sunday, 4 p.m–11 p.m; Monday, closed. Tavern open 24 hours.

Comments: This venerable Italian restaurant is owned by Nevada's current Lieutenant Governor. The joint swings on the weekends with impromptu jamming by such Las Vegas stalwarts as Sonny King.

The Broiler ★★★

Steak/Seafood   Moderate

Boulder Station, Boulder Hwy. and Desert Inn Rd.; (702) 432-7777
Southeast   Zone 5

Dinner: Sunday–Thursday, 5–10 p.m.; Friday and Saturday, 5–11 p.m.

Comments: Fresh seafood, steaks, and prime rib. Reservations should be made for dinner and Sunday brunch.

Brown Derby ★★★★

American   Moderate/Expensive

MGM Grand; (702) 891-7300
Strip   Zone 1

Dinner: Every day, 5:30–10:30 p.m.

Comments: Sit in the Oscar room with its marvelous photographs and feel like a star. Most of the Brown Derby recipes have been adapted well.

Buccaneer Bay Club ★★★★½

Continental   Moderate/Expensive

Treasure Island; (702) 894-7111
Strip   Zone 1

Dinner: Every day, 5–10:30 p.m.

Comments: The menu, geared to the pirate theme, changes seasonally. A rousing sea battle takes place every 90 minutes from 4 p.m. to 11:30 p.m.

Burgundy Room ★★★½

Continental   Moderate/Expensive

Lady Luck Hotel; (702) 477-3000
Downtown   Zone 2

Dinner: Thursday–Monday, 5–11 p.m.

Comments: A moderately expensive gourmet room with a good selection of entrées and fine service in downtown Las Vegas.

Buzios ★★★★

Seafood   Expensive

Rio; (702) 252-7697
Strip   Zone 1

Lunch & Dinner: Every day, 11 a.m.–11 p.m.

(Buzios continued)

Comments: All entrées include a choice of salad or soup. For seafood afficionados Buzios is worth a brief wait, even with a reservation.

Café Nicolle　★★★½

Continental　Moderate

4760 W. Sahara Ave.; (702) 870-7675
Southwest　Zone 3

Lunch & dinner: Monday–Saturday, 11 a.m.–11 p.m.

Comments: This is a longtime local restaurant with a strong local following.

Chang　★★★

Chinese/Dim Sum　Moderate

Gold Key Shopping Center, Strip and Convention Center Dr.
　(702) 731-3388
Strip　Zone 1

Lunch & dinner: Every day, 10 a.m.–midnight. **Dim Sum:** Every day, 10 a.m.–3 p.m.

Comments: Chang shines during the day when owner Hing is on the premises. Special dishes are always available for Chang's Asian customers.

Cheesecake Factory　★★★½

Eclectic　Moderate

The Forum Shops at Caesars Palace; (702) 792-6888
Strip　Zone 1

Lunch & dinner: Monday–Thursday, 11:15 a.m. (after the first Atlantis show)–11:30 p.m.; Friday and Saturday, 11:15 a.m.–12:30 a.m; Sunday, 10:15 a.m.–11:30 p.m.

Comments: The eclectic menu is so large it's spiral-bound. Portions are more than generous. Share a dish rather than forego the cheesecake.

China Grill　★★★★

Asian　Moderate/Expensive

Mandalay Bay; (702) 632-7777
Strip   Zone 1

Dinner: Every day, 5:30–11 p.m.

Comments: Unlike its New York original, the sound level here allows conversation. The comfy lounge is a fine place for relaxing. Food portions are sized to be shared.

Chinois ★★★★
Chinese/French   Moderate/Expensive

The Forum Shops at Caesars Palace; (702) 737-9700
Strip   Zone 1

Lunch & dinner: Every day, 10:30 a.m.–10:30 p.m.

Comments: Chinois is another winner for Puck. The view is wonderful, and the outdoor patio is a fine place for people-watching.

Chungking East ★★
Chinese buffet   Inexpensive

2710 E. Desert Inn Rd.; (702) 693-6883
Southeast   Zone 5

Dinner: Every day, 5–9 p.m.

Comments: The dinner selection includes more seafood and meat dishes; there are more dumplings and vegetables at lunch. The food is always fresh and hot.

Circo (Osteria Del) ★★★½
Italian   Moderate/Expensive

Bellagio; (702) 693-8150
Strip   Zone 1

Dinner: Every day, 5:30–10:30 p.m.

Comments: This elegant Italian restaurant is not as grand as the adjacent Le Cirque, but it's every bit as inviting, and there's super views of the fountain from most tables.

Commander's Palace ★★★★
Creole/Cajun   Expensive

Desert Passage at the Aladdin; (702) 892-8272

(Commander's Palace continued)

Strip   Zone 1

Dinner: Daily, 6–11 p.m.

Comments: Service can sometimes be slow, but the food is always pleasing. Don't expect Café Diablo made tableside. The fire department wouldn't allow it.

Coyote Café   ★★★★
Southwestern   Moderate/Expensive

MGM Grand; (702) 891-7349

Strip   Zone 1

Open: Café: Every day, 8:30 a.m.–11 p.m.; Grill Room: every day, 5:30–10 p.m.

Comments: Mark Miller has defined Southwestern cuisine in his own expert style. Those who like a lighter touch of heat should tell the server.

Delmonico   ★★★★
Steak   Very Expensive

Venetian Hotel; (702) 414-3737

Strip   Zone 1

Dinner: Sunday through Thursday, 5:30–10:30 p.m.; Friday and Saturday, 5:30–11 p.m.

Comments: It's not surprising that owner Emeril Legasse has infused the menu with strong Creole influences. Getting a reservation for prime dinner hours is not easy.

Drai's   ★★★★½
California-Continental   Expensive

Barbary Coast Hotel; (702) 737-0555

Strip   Zone 1

Dinner: Sunday–Thursday, 5:30–10 p.m.; Friday and Saturday, 5:30–11:30 p.m.

Comments: Drai's is a gorgeous new addition to the Barbary Coast. Wednesday through Saturday Drai's becomes an after-hours nightclub—cool and crowded.

8-0-8 ★★★★

Hawaiian/French   Expensive

Caesars Palace; (702) 731-7110
Zone 1

Hours: Sunday, Monday and Thursday, 5:30–10:30 p.m.; Friday and
Saturday, 5:30–11 p.m.

Comments: It's trendy without being chichi, the food and setting are
wonderful. Josselin shows up frequently and is always friendly.

Emeril's New Orleans Fish House ★★★★½

Contemporary New Orleans   Very Expensive

MGM Grand; (702) 891-7777
Strip   Zone 1

Dinner: Every day, 5:30–10:30 p.m.

Comments: Emeril's is an exciting restaurant that personifies the
"new Las Vegas." The food and service are a tribute to Emeril's
concern for his diners.

Fellini's ★★★½

Regional Italian/Provençal   Moderate/Expensive

5555 W. Charleston Blvd.; (702) 870-9999
Southwest   Zone 3

Dinner: Monday–Thursday, 5–10 p.m.; Friday and Saturday, 5–11 p.m.

Comments: Fellini's chef-partner Chaz LaForte spent four years in
Tuscany refining his skills. Free limousine service is offered; just ask for
it when making a reservation.

Ferraro's Restaurant & Lounge ★★★½

Italian   Moderate/Expensive

5900 W. Flamingo Rd.; (702) 364-5300
Southwest   Zone 3
1916 Village Center Circle; (702) 562-9666
North   Zone 5
2895 N Green Valley Pkwy.; (702) 450-5333
North   Zone 5

(Ferraro's Restaurant & Lounge continued)

Flamingo Road:
Dinner: Monday–Sunday, 5:30–10:30 p.m.
Village Center Circle:
Open: Monday–Friday, 11 a.m.–10 p.m.; Saturday, 4–10 p.m.; Sunday,
12–8 p.m.
Green Valley Parkway:
Dinner: Monday–Saturday, 5–10 p.m.; Sunday, 5–9:30 p.m.

Comments: Ferraro's continues to serve southern Italian fare with
some northern Italian specialties.

Fiore   ★★★★

Continental   Moderate/Expensive

Rio; (702) 252-7777
Strip   Zone 1

Dinner: Thursday–Monday, 6–11 p.m. Closed Tuesday and
Wednesday.

Comments: There is much that's new and exciting here; menu
changes are constant.

Florida Café   ★★★½

Cuban   Inexpensive/Moderate

Howard Johnson Hotel, 1481 Las Vegas Blvd. S.; (702) 385-3013
Strip   Zone 1

Dinner: Every day, 4–10 p.m.

Comments: Very little English is spoken here, but the staff is
accommodating and the menu descriptions are clear.

Fortunes   ★★★★

Chinese   Moderate/Expensive

Rio; (702) 247-7923
Strip   Zone 1

Dinner: Tuesday–Saturday, 6–11 p.m.

Comments: It's an experience dining here, but it's not at all
intimidating. Order the live seafood and the bill will rise considerably.

Fuji ★★★

Japanese   Inexpensive/Moderate

3430 E. Tropicana Ave.; (702) 435-8838
Southeast   Zone 5

Dinner: Tuesday–Sunday, 4:30–10 p.m; closed Monday

Comments: Moderate prices, a caring staff, and good food make Fuji a popular local dining option. Children are treated like honored guests.

Garduno's Chili Packing Co. ★★★½

Mexican   Inexpensive/Moderate

Fiesta Hotel; (702) 631-7000
Northwest   Zone 4

Lunch & dinner: Sunday, 10 a.m.–3 p.m., 4–10 p.m.;
Monday–Thursday, 11 a.m.–10 p.m.; Friday and Saturday, 11 a.m.–11 p.m.

Comments: The food is authentic and good. Daily lunch specials are large enough to be an early dinner. The Sunday margarita brunch is a fine value.

Grape Street ★★★½

American bistro and wine bar   Inexpensive/Moderate

Summerhill Plaza, 7501 W. Lake Mead Blvd.; (702) 228-9463
North   Zone 4

Lunch & dinner: Sunday, and Tuesday–Thursday, 11 a.m.–10 p.m.; Friday and Saturday, 11 a.m.–11 p.m.

Comments: Grape Street is a delightful, informal eatery with caring owners. An outdoor patio seats 50. It's always busy.

Harley-Davidson Café ★★★

American Road Food   Moderate

Strip at Harmon; (702) 740-4555
Strip   Zone 1

Hours: Daily, 10 a.m.–midnight

Comments: Be patient, there's usually a line of fans waiting to get their turn. the store is open daily, 9 a.m.–11 p.m. Have fun, you hear.

Habib's ★★★½

Persian/Middle Eastern   Moderate

Sahara Pavilion, 4750 W. Sahara Ave.; (702) 870-0860
Southwest   Zone 3

Dinner: Monday–Saturday, 5–10 p.m.

Comments: Habib's menu is not large, but is filled with exotic dishes that often have unfamiliar names. The wait staff is happy to explain the food.

Hugo's Cellar ★★★½

American   Expensive

Four Queens Hotel; (702) 385-4011
Downtown   Zone 2

Dinner: Every day, 5:30–11 p.m.

Comments: A most popular downtown restaurant. On weekends the Cellar is packed. Expert wine steward to assist you with selection. A consistent local favorite, in spite of too-high prices.

Il Fornaio ★★★

Italian
Moderate/Expensive

New York–New York; (702) 740-6969
Strip   Zone 1

Hours: Everyday, 8:30 a.m.–12 a.m.

Comments: Dine during off hours for the most relaxing experience. Patio dining is the most requested. It can be noisy, though.

Isis ★★★½

Continental   Expensive

Luxor; (702) 262-4773
Strip   Zone 1

Dinner: Thursday–Monday, 5:15–10:45 p.m.; closed Tuesday and Wednesday

Comments: Unusual menu cover decorated with illustrations of Egyptian stone carvings is just one of the original touches at Isis.

Jerusalem ★★½

Middle Eastern/Glatt Kosher   Inexpensive/Moderate

Plaza de Vegas, 1305 Vegas Valley Dr. (East of Maryland Pkwy.)
  (702) 696-1644
Southeast   Zone 5

Lunch & dinner: Sunday–Thursday, 11 a.m.–9 p.m.; Friday, 10 a.m.–3
p.m.; closed Saturday

Comments: Owner Rachel, with 24-hour notice, will make special
dishes. Some inconsistencies exist in the food pricing, but it's mostly a
good value. Portions are large.

Kathy's Southern Cooking ★★★

American   Inexpensive/Moderate

6407 Mountain Vista St.; (702) 433-1005
Southeast   Zone 5

Lunch & dinner: Tuesday–Thursday, 11 a.m.–8:30 p.m.; Friday and
Saturday, 11 a.m.–9:30 p.m.; Sunday, 1–7:30 p.m. Same menu. Closed
Monday.

Comments: The owners of this family operation, Kathy and Felix
Cook, present authentic selections from Mississippi and Louisiana
kitchens.

Kokomo's ★★★★

Seafood/Steak   Expensive

The Mirage; (702) 791-7111
Strip   Zone 1

Dinner: Every day, 5–10:30 p.m.

Comments: Imaginative chefs and decor combine to create a
memorable lunch or dinner in this romantic room.

Lawry's The Prime Rib ★★★½

American   Expensive

4043 Howard Hughes Pkwy.; (702) 893-2223
Strip   Zone 1

Dinner: Sunday–Thursday, 5–10 p.m.; Friday and Saturday, 5–11 p.m.

(Lawry's The Prime Rib continued)

Comments: Lawry's Las Vegas opened with a rush that's never stopped. For prime rib devotees, it's the ultimate luxurious temple of beefdom.

Lindo Michoacan ★★★

Mexican   Moderate

2655 E. Desert Inn Rd.; (702) 735-6828
Southeast   Zone 5

Lunch & dinner: Monday–Wednesday, 11 a.m.–10 p.m.;
Thursday–Sunday, 9 a.m.–11 p.m. Same menu day and evening with lunch specials.

Comments: Lindo Michoacan presents an amazing variety of more than 100 appetizers and entrées, all authentic, a good bet for Mexican food enthusiasts.

Lotus of Siam ★★★½

Thai–Nissan   Moderate/Expensive

Commercial Center, 953 E. Sahara Ave.; (702) 735-3033
Strip   Zone 1

Dinner: Every day, 5:30–9:30 p.m.

Comments: The Issan specialties featured here come from the Northwestern corner of Thailand, bordering Laos. These dishes are both hotter and more highly seasoned than most Thai food.

Magnolia Room ★★★½

Italian/Greek/American   Moderate

Jerry's Nugget Casino; (702) 399-3000
North Las Vegas   Zone 4

Dinner: Wednesday–Saturday, 3–10 p.m.; Sunday, 2–9 p.m.; Monday and Tuesday, closed.

Comments: The Magnolia Room is a real find. The food is not epicurean, but it doesn't pretend to be. An earlier attempt to "get fancy" didn't work.

Makino Sushi Restaurant ★★★★

Japanese   Inexpensive/Moderate

Renaissance Center, Decatur near Flamingo; (702) 889-4477
Southwest   Zone 3

Dinner: 5:30–9 p.m. Monday–Thursday, $20.95; 5:30–10 p.m. Friday;
5–10 p.m. Saturday; 5–9 p.m. Sunday and holidays, $21.95.

Comments: If you enjoy serving yourself, Makino is a fantastic deal.
You'll not find a more appealing array of foods.

Malibu Chan   ★★★★
Pacific Rim   Moderate/Expensive

Promenade Center, 8125 West Sahara; (702) 312-4267
Southwest   Zone 3

Dinner: Everyday, 5 p.m.–2 a.m.

Comments: This high-powered local hangout serves very good,
albeit pricey, food and sushi. The happy hour sushi menu (served 11
pm. until closing) is a terrific value.

Manhattan   ★★★½
Italian   Moderate/Expensive

2600 E. Flamingo Rd.; (702) 737-5000
Strip   Zone 1

Dinner: Everyday, 5 p.m.–1 a.m. (same hours for restaurant and
lounge).

Comments: A separate bar and lounge features a late-night menu
with appetizers, hamburgers, steak sandwiches, and other casual fare.
The dining room menu is also available.

Marrakech   ★★★
Moroccan   Moderate

3900 Paradise Rd.; (702) 736-7655
Strip   Zone 1

Dinner: Every day, 5:30–11 p.m.

Comments: Las Vegas version of Moroccan food in an Arabian
Nights setting. Belly dancing is competent but often intrusive. It's not
authentic, but it's fun.

Mayflower Cuisinier   ★★★★½
Chinese/French   Moderate/Expensive

(Mayflower Cuisinier continued)
4750 W. Sahara Ave.; (702) 870-8432
Southwest   Zone 3

Dinner: Monday–Thursday, 5–9:30 p.m.; Friday and Saturday, 5–10:30 p.m.; Sunday, closed.

Comments: Owner-chef Ming See Woo and manager Theresa, her daughter, created this fine cross-cultural restaurant. An excellent fusion of Chinese and other cuisines.

Michael's   ★★★★
Continental   Very Expensive

Barbary Coast Hotel; (702) 737-7111
Strip   Zone 1

Dinner: Every day, two seatings at 6 and 6:30 p.m., 9 and 9:30 p.m.

Comments: Early diners have a better chance of securing a table than those who like to dine at prime time.

Mon Ami Gabi   ★★★★
French Steakhouse   Moderate/Expensive

Paris Hotel; (702) 944-GABI
Strip   Zone 1

Dinner: Sunday–Thursday, 5–11 p.m. Friday and Saturday, 5 p.m.–12 a.m.

Comments: Mon Ami is a charming dining place. everyone wants to dine at the sidewalk café, but you'll have to come early to get a table (there are no reservations for the café).

Mortoni's   ★★★½
Italian, California-style   Moderate/Expensive

Hard Rock Hotel; (702) 693-5000
Strip   Zone 1

Dinner: Sunday, Monday and Thursday, 6–10 p.m.; Friday and Saturday, 6–11 p.m.; Tuesday and Wednesday, closed.

Comments: Only natural ingredients and organic produce are used at Mortoni's. The menu is small but choice, offering a full selection of dishes.

Morton's   ★★★½
Steak   Very Expensive

400 East Flamingo Rd.; (702) 893-0703
Strip   Zone 1

Dinner: Monday–Thursday, 5:30–11 p.m.; Friday and Saturday, 5–11 p.m; Sunday, 5–10 p.m.

Comments: Appetizers, salads, entrées, desserts all served à la carte in large portions. The dessert soufflés are a specialty but disappointing.

Napa   ★★★★★
Contemporary French cuisine   Expensive

Rio; (702) 252-7777
Strip   Zone 1

Dinner: Tuesday–Saturday, 6–11 p.m.

Comments: Celebrity chef Jean-Louis Palladin works in an exhibition kitchen that can be viewed from the front tables.

Neros   ★★★★
Contemporary American   Expensive

Caesars Palace; (702) 731-7731
Strip   Zone 1

Dinner: Every day, 5:30–11 p.m.

Comments: This one-time steak house took on new life under former Chef Mario Capone, formerly of Biba restaurant in Boston.

Noodles   ★★★½
Chinese/Japanese/Thai/Vietnamese   Moderate

Bellagio; (702) 693-7111
Strip   Zone 1

Hours: Sunday–Thursday, 11 a.m.–11 p.m.; Friday and Saturday, 11 a.m.–2 a.m.

Comments: Noodles is small, only 88 seats, so it's tough to get in at prime times, but it's open long hours so you're bound to get in sometime.

Olio ★★★½

Contemporary Italian   Moderate/Expensive

MGM Grand; (702) 891-7775

Strip   Zone 1

Hours: Lunch and dinner, Sunday–Thursday, 11 a.m.–midnight; Friday and Saturday, 11:30 a.m.–2 a.m.

Comments: Olio has so much going it can make you gaga. Prices are moderate at the antipasto bar, more costly in the dining rooms.

Olives ★★★★

American/Mediterranean   Moderate/Expensive

Bellagio; (702) 693-7223

Strip   Zone 1

Dinner: Every day, 5–11:30 p.m.

Comments: Olives at Bellagio bears no resemblance to the Boston original, but it does have the same warmth and expert staff.

The Palm ★★★★

Steak   Very Expensive

The Forum Shops at Caesars Palace; (702) 732-7256

Strip   Zone 1

Dinner: Every day, 11:30 a.m.–10:30 p.m.

Comments: Caters to celebrities, with drawings of many entertainers and local movers and shakers on the walls. The Palm suffers from good fortune—too much business.

Pamplemousse ★★★½

Continental/French   Expensive

400 E. Sahara Ave.; (702) 733-2066

Strip   Zone 1

Dinner: Tuesday–Sunday, 6–10 p.m.; Monday, closed.

Comments: Waiters will give prices when reciting menu only if asked. Ask, so there are no surprises when the check arrives.

Pasta Pirate

★★★½

Seafood/Pasta   Moderate

California Hotel; (702) 385-1222
Downtown   Zone 2

Dinner: Every day, 5:30–11 p.m.

Comments: The Pasta Pirate offers an imaginative menu at moderate prices. Consistently good food and prices.

Peking Market

★★★½

Chinese   Moderate

Flamingo Hilton; (702) 733-3111
Strip   Zone 1

Dinner: Friday–Tuesday, 5:30–11 p.m.; Wednesday and Thursday, closed.

Comments: Peking Market has posh new decor, an expanded staff for better service, and an extensive menu of regional Chinese dishes.

Pho Chien

★★★½

Vietnamese   Inexpensive/Moderate

3839 West Sahara; (702) 873-8749
Southwest   Zone 3

Lunch & dinner: Monday, Tuesday, Thursday, and Friday, 10:30 a.m.–9 p.m.; Wednesday, 10 a.m.–4 p.m.; Saturday and Sunday, 10:30 a.m.–10 p.m.

Comments: The food is far prettier than the premises, and it's very good. This is not capital "D" dining, but if you're in the mood for a delicious, inexpensive meal served quickly, this is the place.

Picasso

★★★★★

French with Spanish influence   Expensive/Very Expensive

Bellagio; (702) 693-7223
Strip   Zone 1

Dinner: Thursday–Tuesday, 6–9:30 p.m; Wednesday, closed.

Comments: This exceptional restaurant is grand yet unpretentious.

Piero's   ★★★★½

Italian   Expensive

355 Convention Center Dr.; (702) 369-2305

Strip   Zone I

Dinner: Every day, 5:30–9 p.m.

Comments: Celebrities and sports figures always make their way to Piero's, as do Las Vegas power brokers, who consistently dine here.

Pinot Brasserie   ★★★½

French   Moderate/Expensive

Venetian Hotel; (702) 414-8888

Strip   Zone I

Dinner: Sunday–Thursday, 5:30–10 p.m.; Friday and Saturday, 5:30–10:30 p.m.

Comments: A small café outside the Brasserie is a fine place to people-watch and enjoy a casual meal. They serve seafood, appetizers, sandwiches, salads, and some entrées—but it's plenty to choose from.

Prime   ★★★★½

Steakhouse   Expensive

Bellagio; (702) 693-8484

Strip   Zone I

Dinner: Every day, 5:30–11 p.m.

Comments: Prime is on the lower level of the shopping corridor beside Picasso. Both restaurants get their share of lookers, but the staff keeps them from disturbing diners. It's hard to resist this rare steakhouse.

Rainforest Café   ★★★½

American   Moderate

MGM Grand; (702) 891-8580

Strip   Zone I

Lunch & dinner: Every day, 10:30 a.m. until closing: Monday–Thursday and Sunday, until 11 p.m.; Friday and Saturday, until midnight

Comments: Themed restaurants are very common in Las Vegas, but

Rainforest Café has better food than most, and a wonderful theme.
Ask about the free safari tours.

Range Steakhouse   ★★★½

American   Expensive

Harrah's; (702) 369-5000
Strip   Zone 1

Dinner: Sunday–Thursday, 5:30–10:30 p.m.; Friday and Saturday, 5:30–
11:30 p.m.; bar open until 2 a.m.

Comments: The Range is a prime example of the direction Harrah's
has taken. An elegant lounge and bar serves light snacks. An ideal spot
for viewing the action on the Strip.

Red Square   ★★★½

American/"Russian"   Expensive

Mandalay Bay; (702) 632-7777
Strip   Zone 1

Dinner: Every night, 5:30 p.m.–midnight; bar open Sunday–Thursday
until 2 a.m. and until 4 a.m. Friday and Saturday

Comments: Another winning concept from the China Grill creators.
There are some dining limits, ask when you make your reservation.

Redwood Bar & Grill   ★★★½

American/Prime Rib   Moderate

(Redwood bar & Grill continued)
California Hotel.; (702) 385-1222
Downtown   Zone 2

Dinner: Every day, 5:30–11 p.m.

Comments: Excellent value. Prime rib portion is succulent,
generous, and cooked as ordered. Outstanding value.

Renoir   ★★★★★

French/American   Very Expensive

Mirage; (702) 791-7111
Strip   Zone 1

Dinner: Tuesday–Sunday, 6–10 p.m.; closed Mondays.

(Renoir continued)

Comments: Flawless food and service in a divine setting, yet it's not terribly pretentious. A genuinely welcoming staff adds to the charm and your comfort level.

Ricardo's ★★★½

Mexican   Moderate

4930 W. Flamingo Rd.; (702) 871-7119
Southwest   Zone 3

2380 E. Tropicana Ave.; (702) 798-4515
Southeast   Zone 5

MGM Grand; (702) 736-4970
Strip   Zone 1

Lunch & dinner: Same menu day and evening, all locations.

West Flamingo Road: Friday–Saturday, 11 a.m.–11 p.m.; Monday–Thursday, 11 a.m.–10 p.m.
East Tropicana Avenue: Monday–Thursday, 11 a.m.–10 p.m.; Friday–Saturday, 11 a.m.–11 p.m.
MGM Grand: Every day, 11 a.m.–11 p.m.; until 2:30 a.m. Fridays and Saturdays (with entertainment)

Comments: Although all the restaurants are operated by the same owners, each restaurant has its own distinctive flavor and specials.

Ristorante Italiano ★★★½

Italian   Expensive

Riviera Hotel; (702) 734-5110
Strip   Zone 1

Dinner: Friday–Tuesday, 5:30–10 p.m.; Wednesday and Thursday, closed.

Comments: Menu includes contemporary dishes as well as a good classic Italian selection. A private dining room, which is warm and inviting, is available for small parties.

Rosewood Grille ★★★½

Lobster/Steak   Expensive

3339 Las Vegas Blvd., S.; (702) 792-9099
Strip   Zone 1

Dinner: Every day, 4:30–11:30 p.m.

Comments: Restaurant stocks a week's supply of large and extra-large lobsters (up to 25 pounds). Price (three-pound minimum) changes with the market. Lobster prices are typically $17–22 per pound, depending on availability.

Rumjungle ★★★½

Brazilian rodizio/nightclub — Moderate/Expensive

Mandalay Bay; (702) 632-7408

Strip Zone 1

Dinner: Monday–Thursday, 5:30–11 p.m.; Friday and Saturday, 5:30 p.m. to last seating (usually 9 p.m.)

Comments: There are many rules and restrictions here. On weekends, parties of eight or more have two hours in which to dine. There is a cover charge after 11 p.m. Still, rumjungle is a cool spot for the younger set.

Ruth's Chris Steak House ★★★★

Steak — Expensive

3900 Paradise Rd.; (702) 791-7011

Strip Zone 1

4561 W. Flamingo Rd.; (702) 248-7011

Southwest Zone 5

Dinner: **Paradise:** Every day, 4:30–10:30 p.m.; Flamingo: 4:30 p.m.–3 a.m.

Comments: Wine selection includes Dom Perignon and Louis Roederer Cristal, in the $100- to $300-per-bottle category. Ruth's Chris serves only prime beef.

Sam Woo Bar-B-Q ★★★

Chinese Barbecue — Inexpensive

Chinatown Mall, 4215 Spring Mountain Rd.; (702) 368-7628

Southwest Zone 3

Lunch & dinner: Every day, 10 a.m.–5 a.m. Take-out barbecue shop: Every day, 10 a.m.–10 p.m.

Comments: Very little English is spoken here, but the menu is in English. Service is good but brusque when the restaurant is busy.

Samba Grill ★★★★

Brazilian steakhouse   Moderate

Mirage; (702) 791-7111

Strip   Zone 1

Dinner: Every day, 5:30–10:15 p.m.(last seating)

Comments: The jewel-like bar is a nice place for appetizers. Samba Grill is a terrific new restaurant with prices right out of Old Las Vegas.

Sazio ★★★½

Italian   Moderate

Orleans Hotel, Valley View and Arville; (702) 948-9501

Southwest   Zone 3

Dinner: Daily, 11 a.m.–11 p.m.

Comments: Sazio is a terrific value. Food may be ordered solo, for one person, or grandioso, for family-style platters.

Seasons ★★★★

Continental   Very Expensive

Bally's; (702) 739-4111

Strip   Zone 1

Dinner: Tuesday–Saturday, 6–11 p.m.; Sunday and Monday, closed.

Comments: Bally's featured gourmet room. Menu reflects today's demand for lighter, healthier dining. A new French chef is making waves with the menu; it's lighter and more varied.

Sir Galahad's ★★★½

Prime rib   Moderate

Excalibur; (702) 597-7777

Strip   Zone 1

Dinner: Sunday–Thursday, 5–10 p.m. (last seating); Friday and Saturday, 5–11 p.m. (last seating)

Comments: Prime rib plus Yorkshire pudding, creamed spinach, mashed potatoes, and beef barley soup or green salad is a very hearty meal.

Spago ★★★★★

American   Moderate/Expensive

The Forum Shops at Caesars Palace; (702) 369-6300
Strip   Zone 1

Dinner: Every day, 6–9:30 p.m.

Comments: Wolfgang Puck's first venture outside California is an
instant success. Puck surrounds himself with the best staff, the best
ingredients, the best of everything.

Star Canyon ★★★½

Southwestern   Moderate/Expensive

Venetian Hotel; phone (702) 414-3772
Strip   Zone 1

Dinner: Sunday–Thursday, 5:30–10 p.m.; Friday and Saturday, 6–11
p.m.

Comments: Everything from omelettes to barbecued beef
sandwiches to wood-roasted Maine lobster gets equal attention.

The Steak House ★★★½

Steak   Moderate

Circus Circus; (702) 734-0410
Strip   Zone 1

Dinner: Monday–Friday, 5–11 p.m.; Saturday, 5 p.m.–midnight

Comments: Consistently high quality and service. Don't be fooled
by the children running around the lobby. Inside the Steak House, the
atmosphere is adult and the food is wonderful.

Stefano's ★★★★

Southern Italian   Moderate/Expensive

Golden Nugget; (702) 385-7111
Downtown   Zone 2

Dinner: Sunday–Thursday, 6–10:30 p.m.; Friday and Saturday, 5:30–
10:30 p.m.

Comments: Dishes presented with flair. A happy dining experience.

Swiss Café   ★★★½

European   Moderate

3250 E. Tropicana Ave.; (702) 454-2270
Southeast   Zone 5

Dinner: Monday–Saturday, 5–10 p.m.

Comments: Chef-owner Wolfgang and his wife-partner, Mary,
welcome everyone. The affable couple have a devoted local following.

Terrazza   ★★★★½

Italian   Expensive

Caesars Palace; (702) 731-7110
Strip   Zone 1

Dinner: Every day, 5:30–10:30 p.m.

Comments: Terrazza in the new Palace Tower has replaced the older
Primavera. The main dining room is adjacent to Terrazza's lounge,
where diners may have a before-dinner drink and a variety of pizzas
and focaccia.

Teru Sushi   ★★★½

Sushi   Moderate/Expensive

700 E. Sahara Ave.; (702) 734-6655
Strip   Zone 1

Dinner: Monday–Saturday, 5–11 p.m.; closed Sunday.

Comments: Sushi-quality fish is the best, and here it is priced
accordingly. Portions are Japanese-style—small.

The Tillerman   ★★★½

Seafood   Moderate/Expensive

2245 E. Flamingo Rd.; (702) 731-4036
Southeast   Zone 5

Dinner: Sunday–Thursday, 5–10 p.m.; Friday and Saturday, 5–11 p.m.

Comments: One of the most popular Las Vegas seafood restaurants.
A new owner has made many improvements. For the first time since
opening, the Tillerman accepts reservations.

Tokyo   ★★★½
Japanese/Sushi   Moderate

Commercial Center, 953 E. Sahara Ave.; (702) 735-7070
Strip   Zone 1

Dinner: Every day, 5–10 p.m.

Comments: A family-run restaurant—very popular with the locals.
Tokyo has been enlarged to include party and catering facilities.

Top of the World   ★★★½
American   Expensive

Stratosphere Tower.; (702) 380-7711
Strip   Zone 1

Dinner: Sunday–Thursday, 6–11 p.m.; Friday and Saturday, 6 p.m.–
midnight.

Comments: The food is secondary to the view, which is simply
spectacular, but the food is very good. There is a $15 food minimum.

Trattoria del Lupo   ★★★★
Italian   Moderate/Expensive

Mandalay Bay; (702) 740-5522
Strip   Zone 1

Dinner: 5–11 p.m. Sunday–Thursday; Friday and Saturday 5
p.m.–midnight

Comments: Executive chef Mark Ferguson came to Lupo from Spago
after a tour of Italy. Lupo is a cool dining place.

Venetian   ★★★½
Italian   Moderate/Expensive

3713 W. Sahara Ave.; (702) 876-4190
Southwest   Zone 3

(Venetian continued)

Open: Every day, 24 hours (dinner, 4–11 p.m.).

Comments: Portions are generous, and the menu is extensive.
Longtime diners are hoping it remains that way.

Viva Mercado's ★★★½

Mexican   Moderate

6128 W. Flamingo Rd.; (702) 871-8826
Southwest   Zone 3

Town Center (adjacent to Barley's Sunset); (702) 435-6200
Southeast   Zone 5

Lunch & dinner: Same menu day and evening, all locations.

West Flamingo Road: Sunday–Thursday, 11 a.m.–9:30 p.m.;
Friday–Saturday, 11 a.m.–10:30 p.m.
Town Center: Sunday–Thursday, 11 a.m.–9:30 p.m.; Friday–Saturday,
11 a.m.–10 p.m.

Comments: The owner created a number of the entrées. In keeping
with today's healthier lifestyle, he cooks exclusively with canola oil.

VooDoo Café & Lounge ★★★½

Creole/Cajun   Moderate/Expensive

Rio Hotel; (702) 252-7777
Strip   Zone 1

Hours: Every day, 5–11 p.m.

Comments: It took a while for VooDoo to hit its stride, but now this
colorful eatery and late-night hangout offers some very tasty food.

Wild Sage Café ★★★

Contemporary American   Moderate/Expensive

600 West Warm Springs, (McKaren Shopping center); (702) 944-7243
Need Zone

Dinner: Sunday–Thursday, 5–9:30 p.m.; Friday and Saturday, 5–10 p.m.

Comments: Owned by Spago alumni, these young chefs really know
how to cook. Service can be slow, but that's because most items are
cooked to order, so be patient.

Wolfgang Puck Café ★★★½

American   Moderate

MGM Grand; (702) 891-3019
Strip   Zone 1

Breakfast, lunch & dinner: Sunday–Thursday, 8 a.m.–11 p.m.; Friday and Saturday, 8–1 a.m.

Comments: When busy, as it usually is, service can be slow, and food quality inconsistent. Sidewalk café design allows diners to watch people in the MGM Grand's casino.

Index

Unofficial Guide **Reader Survey**

If you would like to express your opinion about Las Vegas or this guide-book, complete the following survey and mail it to:

> *Unofficial Guide* Reader Survey
> PO Box 43673
> Birmingham AL 35243

Inclusive dates of your visit: _____

*Members of
your party:* Person 1   Person 2   Person 3   Person 4   Person 5

Gender: M F   M F   M F   M F   M F

Age: _____

Have you ever been to Las Vegas before? _____
Was this your first trip to Las Vegas? _____
On your most recent trip, where did you stay? _____

Concerning your accommodations, on a scale of 100 as best and 0 as worst, how would you rate:

The quality of your room?   ____   The value of your room?   ____
The quietness of your room?   ____   The reservation process?   ____
Staff's relations with foreigners? ____ Overall hotel satisfaction? ____

Did you use public transportation? _____   What kind? _____

Concerning public transportation, on a scale of 100 as best and 0 as worst, how would you rate:

Ease of use?   ____   Value vs. rental cars?   ____
Cleanliness?   ____   Hours and areas serviced?   ____
Airport shuttle efficiency? ____

Concerning your dining experiences:

Estimate the number of meals eaten in restaurants per day: _____
Approximately how much did your party spend on meals per day? ____
Favorite restaurants in Las Vegas: _____
_____

Did you buy this guide before leaving? ☐   While on your trip? ☐

How did you hear about this guide? (check all that apply)

Loaned or recommended by a friend ☐   Radio or TV ☐
Newspaper or magazine ☐   Bookstore salesperson   ☐
Just picked it out on my own ☐   Library ☐
Internet ☐

Unofficial Guide Reader Survey (continued)

What other guidebooks did you use on this trip? _____

_____

_____

_____

On a scale of 100 as best and 0 as worst, how would you rate them?

_____

_____

_____

Using the same scale, how would you rate *The Unofficial Guide(s)?*

_____

Are *Unofficial Guides* readily available at bookstores in your area? _____

Have you used other *Unofficial Guides?* _____

Which one(s)? _____

_____

_____

_____

_____

Comments about your Las Vegas trip or *The Unofficial Guide(s):*

_____

_____

_____

_____

_____

_____

_____

_____

_____

_____

_____

_____

_____